God
Loves
Women

Scarlett Harrington

Heather,
God Bless You
Richly,
Scarlett Harrington

paige 1
PUBLISHING

All scripture is quoted from *The King James Version* of the Bible unless otherwise noted.

Scripture quotations marked NJKV are taken from *The New King James Version* copyright ©1982 by Thomas Nelson, Inc. Used by Permission. All Rights Reserved.

Scripture quotations taken from the Amplified® Bible, Copyright © 1954, 1958, 1962, 1964, 1965, 1987 by The Lockman Foundation. Used by permission. **www.Lockman.org**

Scripture quotations taken from the *New American Standard Bible*®, Copyright © 1960, 1962, 1963, 1968, 1971, 1972, 1973, 1975, 1977, 1995 by The Lockman Foundation. Used by permission. **www.Lockman.org**

God Loves Women
Scarlett Harrington
ISBN: 978-0-9819879-7-2

Published by Paige1 Publishing
Tulsa, Oklahoma
www.Paige1Publishing.com

Table of Contents

Introduction

God first began to deal with me on the topic of women sometime ago as I was preparing to teach a message on God's willingness to heal the physical body. On this occasion, I was reading in Mark 5:25-30 where the verses describe Jesus ministering to the woman with the issue of blood. You'll recall that she had suffered many things of many physicians, but only grew worse. Ultimately, the woman heard of Jesus and came and touched the hem of His garment and immediately virtue flowed out of Jesus to heal her.

As I read this powerful passage, the Spirit of God spoke to me specifically about the word *virtue* in verse 30. Actually, as I read those words, the Lord spoke in my heart, asking, "Do you know the meaning of *virtue?*"

"Well, I think it means power," I replied.

Immediately He reminded me of Proverbs 31:11 and said, "Do you know that a virtuous woman is a powerful woman?"

His simple yet profound questions led me into a new study that altogether changed my perspective of the virtuous woman. Without realizing it, I had developed the misconception that the virtuous woman of Proverbs 31 was weak, mousy, and introverted. I imagined her as a woman who seldom set aside her hobbies of cooking and sewing. In many ways, she seemed outdated and out of touch compared to the woman of today. Unfortunately, I did not relate to her nor did I desire to be like her.

But as God began to reveal to me the power this virtuous woman possessed, my opinion of her changed dramatically. I became engrossed in her lifestyle and overwhelmed with her remarkable accomplishments and outstanding qualities. In fact, as I began to study and meditate on this text, I grew more and more astounded by the woman's strength and power. I began to realize that she demonstrated an incredible love for her family and attained an extraordinary level of financial prosperity all the while tremendously impacting her community. I began to desire this very same kind of power in my own life. Most importantly, I began to realize that this same virtue—defined as strength, might, force and wealth—is available to every woman who remains vitally attached to Jesus.

Proverbs 31:29 says, "Many daughters have done virtuously, but thou excellest them all." Of all the women in the

Old Testament who did mighty exploits for God—including Sarah, Deborah, Abigail, Ruth, Esther, and Hannah to name a few—God said this virtuous woman "excellest" them all. Wow, what mighty power she possessed.

I pray as you read the pages of this book, you also will begin to comprehend God's profound love for women, and His intense desire to empower His daughters. Most of all, I pray that God will reveal to you how very powerful you are in Christ Jesus.

Chapter One

Finding a Virtuous Woman

Who can find a virtuous woman?

Proverbs 31:10

The Bible is filled with magnificent questions. Jesus Himself asked a lot of questions and answered His critics with questions. Here the writer of Proverbs asks a particularly important question: Who can find a virtuous woman?

Even the question itself contributes important information by implying that it might not be an easy task to find a virtuous woman. After all, her price is far above rubies, suggesting she is a rare find.

Nevertheless, some harbor misconceptions of what characterizes a virtuous woman. There are those who read Proverbs

31 and say, "I cannot possibly attain to this level of perfection. Who can live up to the performance of this woman of virtue?" There are others who wonder where the woman of Proverbs 31 finds her energy and stamina. Still other women resent the virtuous woman for raising such a high standard for the rest of us to attain.

However, as we gain understanding of God's plan for women, we can clearly see that it is God who enables and equips His daughters to do His will. As women we are not left in our own strength to push, struggle, and strive to be everything to everybody. God Himself empowers us to accomplish all we do, and in the process He adds great joy to our lives and imparts even greater beauty and strength to us.

Frankly, too many women have been religiously brainwashed instead of biblically taught. You see, the word *virtuous* does not mean perfect; it means powerful. Therefore, the simple yet profound truth is that a virtuous woman is a woman full of God's power.

As the Holy Spirit reveals His purposes for women, we discover how simple it is to operate in this same fashion. Women of all ages can join the prestigious rank of being virtuous women.

The Meaning of *Virtuous*

While reading and studying to prepare a sermon on the subject of healing from Mark 5, the Holy Spirit revealed a truth to me. The Bible says the woman with the issue of blood came in the press behind and touched the hem of Jesus' garment, for she said, "If I may touch but his garment, I shall be whole." Jesus acknowledged something flowed from him to this woman of faith.

In Mark 5:30 He says, "Immediately knowing in himself that **virtue** had gone out of him, [Jesus] turned … about in the press, and said Who touched my clothes?" Virtue was released to her. It entered her physical body and brought about total recovery.

When I read the word *virtue*, the Holy Spirit spoke to me and said, "Do you know the meaning of virtue?"

"Well, I think it means power," I replied.

Immediately, He took me to Proverbs 31, where He opened my eyes to see this very powerful woman in a new and different way. He also shared with me His intention to make all women strong. Why?

God loves women.

God is not a male chauvinist. He does not oppress women, nor does He treat them with any less respect than He treats men. In fact, God moved on Peter to write that men ought to give honor to their wives with tenderness or their prayers will be hindered. I like to put it this way: God will not even talk to husbands who treat their wives dishonorably (1 Peter 3:7). God wants a man to love his wife, to nourish her, and to cherish her (Ephesians 5:29).

Jesus also loves women. He came to set them free and liberate them. Jesus elevates women to a place of honor and respect. Again and again, recorded in the Gospels, Jesus shows His great love for women as He encourages and ministers to them. He empowers them for works of service.

Jesus came to show us the Father and said, "He that hath seen me, hath seen the Father" (John 14:9). He said "I do nothing of myself, but as my Father hath taught me, I speak those things" (John 8:28). As we see the love and compassion that Jesus displays toward women, we understand how God feels about them.

While attending a wedding, Jesus submitted to the request of His mother and performed the first miracle. How interesting that the faith of a woman actually activated the first miracle of our Lord Jesus. She simply asked Jesus to do something and then told the servants to do whatever He asked them to do (John 2:5).

Before the Lord brought revelation to me, I perceived the virtuous woman to be an extremely talented cook, preparing gourmet meals for her family. I pictured her in my mind as Betty Crocker or Rachel Ray. I thought she was a terrific seamstress. It seemed as though her life was perfect. At that point, I also believed a virtuous woman was required to be married with children.

But one by one I began to discover that these were half truths. The only other woman in the entire Bible that was referred to as a virtuous was Ruth. In fact, Boaz said to Ruth, "For all the city of my people doeth know that thou art a virtuous woman" (Ruth 3:11). Yet, at the time, Ruth was a single woman who was widowed with no children and no money. She did have a bitter mother-in-law named Naomi. Ruth was from Moab, and in some people's minds, she was even of the "wrong race." Why would they call her virtuous?

The definition of *virtuous* found in Strong's Exhaustive Concordance of the Bible surprised me[1]. *Virtuous* means strong, mighty, efficient, able, wealthy, forceful, and with substance. This multi-word description shed new light on the word for me. I began to understand how this kind of power flows only from the all-powerful One, our heavenly Father, the omnipotent God. Suddenly I realized that the reason Ruth was known as a virtuous woman was explained by Boaz in the preceding verse where he said to Ruth, "Blessed thou of the Lord" (Ruth 3:1).

Ruth truly was blessed and empowered by God. How do we know it is true? Because in Ruth 1:16, Ruth said to Naomi, "Thy people shall be my people, **thy God my God**." When she chose God, she became virtuous; she became powerful. When we choose God, we also become virtuous and powerful. As we live in Him, we have access to all that He is.

God's power is different from the world's power or the devil's, and it is far greater. Jesus said, "Behold, I give thee power to tread on serpents and scorpions and over all the power of the enemy and nothing shall by any means hurt thee" (Luke 10:19).

The God-kind of power is always based in love and never selfishness. Therefore, God's idea of a virtuous and powerful woman is not a manipulative, scheming, selfish, controlling woman. That description does characterize the world's image of a powerful woman, and it also sounds very much like another woman we read about in the Bible named Jezebel. Jezebel was strong all right; but not strong in God. She was not submitted to God, and she was very strong willed.

After all, she even ruled over King Ahab, her husband, and commanded hundreds of the prophets of Baal (1 Kings 18:19). The woman was the very opposite of the Proverbs 31 woman and was the very definition of manipulation and control. She sent a bold threat to God's prophet Elijah through her servant threatening to kill him. Jezebel was bold enough to mock God Himself in 1 Kings 19:2.

There was great evil in Jezebel's heart, and in 1 Kings 21:1-29 she schemed to kill Naboth. At issue was a plot of land that King Ahab desired. The problem was that the land belonged to Naboth, who refused to sell or trade the land that had been in his family for many years. Ahab was distraught, so Jezebel intervened and sent letters to the people, forging Ahab's signature. She set up two false witnesses against Naboth that testified before the people, and the witnesses testified that Naboth blasphemed God. The king ordered Naboth out of the city, and the people stoned him. Jezebel told Ahab to go possess Naboth's vineyard.

The Bible states in 1 Kings 21:25 that King Ahab sold himself to work wickedness in the sight of the Lord, whom Jezebel his wife stirred up or inspired him to do. From the world's perspective this woman had power and influence, but it was not the power of God. This selfish evil power was rooted in the devil; God's power is far greater and rooted and grounded in love, which never fails (1 Corinthians 13:8).

Women like Jezebel—and there are plenty of them around even today—feel they must dominate, control, and manipulate. These women are driven by fear and insecurity, which make them only weaker. There's no happily ever after for women who pursue this selfish behavior. The real truth is that strength stems from faith in God, and courage is derived from trusting in Him.

In 2 Kings 9 we read of Jezebel's unhappy demise. She was thrown out of a window and her body was eaten by dogs, just as Elijah had prophesied. All that was left of her was her skull, her feet and the palms of her hands. It was not a pretty ending for Jezebel to become dog food.

Jezebel's life was an example of Proverbs 14:12 that says, "There is a way that seemeth right unto a man, but the end thereof are the ways are of death (destruction)." She followed a path that was not right unto God, but right to her. And she paid for it with her life.

Contentious, nagging women like Jezebel are repulsive. Indeed, Proverbs states two times that it is better to dwell in the corner of the housetop, than with a brawling woman in a wide house (Proverbs 21:9, Proverbs 25:24). Instead of trusting God and believing in Him to move and supply for them, fear forces some women into continually nagging to get things accomplished or to get their way.

Unfortunately, fear only opens the door to the enemy or the devil. Foolish women pluck their houses down (Psalms 53:1). What constitutes a fool? Psalms 53:1 says, "A fool says in his heart, *there is* no God." A fool acts like God is not real, not alive. A fool disregards God in her life. A fool acts like the Word of God is not true.

If you remove the italicized words in Psalm 53:1 that were added by the liberty of the translators, it actually reads "A fool says…no God." A fool will say no to God, no to His Word, no to His instruction, no to His plan. Help us Lord, not to be a foolish woman like Jezebel.

But when we set our love upon our heavenly Father, we become established in Him and shall not be moved. We are unshakeable when we trust in the living God—rock solid. As we trust in Him, we become strong in the Lord and in the power of His might that cannot be defeated (Ephesians 6:10).

The Strongest Force on Earth

What is the strongest force on the earth?

Love.

The Bible says that love never fails (1 Corinthians 13:8, AMP).

Love is a force that cannot be reckoned with, and it's the strongest energy in the universe.

First John 4:7 states, "God is love." Notice the Bible does not say God is power or God is wisdom. Of course we know God has power and has wisdom, but He *is* love. The God-kind of love is agape and unconditional. It also never fails, and since we know God is love, we also know He never fails.

Therefore, a woman who is strong in the Lord is also of love, and because she walks in this love she cannot fail. The Bible says that faith works by love, and when it is coupled with wisdom, it builds. So we understand that a wise woman builds her house (Psalms 53:1), and a house built on love can stand strong and true no matter what goes on around it.

We also need power to overcome even though the world is full of power struggles. We hear about these struggles as we listen to news broadcasts of turmoil and discord throughout the world. We find power struggles in our own politics and country. We find this contention in our state governments, in our local governments, in our churches, in our workplaces and in our homes.

Yet, as God imparts His love to us, we actually receive a whole lot more. For one thing, power comes with it. Second Timothy 1:7 opens our eyes to all that God's love includes when it says, "God hath not given us the spirit of fear; but of **power**, and of love, and of a sound mind. As we walk in God's love, we are equipped to be the most powerful people on the earth. God qualifies this statement by emphasizing the importance of power being mixed with love and a sound and healthy mind.

Where does this power come from and where is it to be used? Acts 1:8 states, "But you shall receive **power** after that the Holy Ghost is come upon you and ye shall be witness unto me." Jesus said, "Behold, I give you **power** to tread on serpents and scorpions and over all the power of the enemy and nothing shall by any means hurt you" (Luke 10:19). Acts 10:38 states, "How God anointed Jesus of Nazareth with the Holy Ghost and with **power**: who went about doing good, and healing all that were oppressed of the devil; for God was with him."

God desires women to be powerful in Him; He doesn't want weak daughters. He said let the weak say I am strong (Joel 3:10). He is a mighty God, and He wants mighty children. It's time for us to acknowledge every good thing in us, so that we may become effective (Philemon 1:6).

Clearly, powerful godly women must depend upon the Holy Ghost. Mary, the mother of Jesus, asked the angel that appeared to her to tell her she would bear a son, "How shall this be, seeing I know not a man?" She wanted to know how a miracle was going to take place. The angel answered saying, "The Holy Ghost shall come…" (Luke 1:34).

You see, the Holy Ghost is the power of God. He is the anointing of God and the hand of God—the One who brings things to pass. The Holy Ghost came and caused a miracle to be done. The Holy Ghost overshadowed Mary, and she conceived Jesus. Too often we Christians look to the natural realm for help instead of looking to God for strength. The source of our strength does not come from man, but from God. We do not need to look to the hand of man for help, but to the hand of God.

The virtuous woman looked to God as her source and trusted in Him, and that's why she is a valuable and worthy role model of virtue for all women.

Virtuous Means Wealthy

> *Her price is far above rubies….*
>
> *Proverbs 31:10*

Our Proverbs 31 text tells us that the value of the virtuous woman is far above rubies, which is a very great price.

For thousands of years rubies have been considered the most valuable gemstone on the earth. They offer magnificent color, and they are associated with love, vivacity, passion, and power. These gems have excellent hardness and outstanding brilliance. Rubies with their finer qualities are extremely rare.

The red color of a fine ruby is incomparable. Some say it represents fire and blood, warmth and life for mankind. Rare rubies are hot with passion and powerful in color.[2] The Bible exhorts us to be fervent (red hot) in spirit. Revelation 3:15-16 states that God would rather us be hot or cold than lukewarm. I know it is God's will for us to become fully mature in Christ and be fervent women who fulfill all the plan of God.

No wonder these characteristics describe virtuous, Christian women. We are magnificent, powerful, outstanding, and brilliant.

Chapter 2

A Virtuous Woman
Loves her Husband

The heart of her husband doeth safely trust in her, so that he shall have no need of spoil. Proverbs 31:11

Proverbs 18:22 says, "Whoso findeth a good wife, findeth a good thing, and obtaineth favour of the Lord." The Bible speaks boldly of God's love for women as it declares to men that when they find a good wife they obtain favor or pleasure, delight, goodwill, and acceptance from God.

Yet notice that the scripture uses the word *wife*, not woman. Why is this? The reason is because women must learn how to be good wives—it's not automatic. Actually, in Titus 2:3-5, older women are encouraged to instruct the young women to be wise and *how* to love their husbands and love their children.

One would not think you would have to teach women how to love their husbands and children, but obviously God knows better. The Word of God advises us to renew our mind to love God's way, which far surpasses "human love" or even a "mother's love."

A part of loving is to be trustworthy; there can be no intimacy without trust. Trust is vital to any relationship, so the virtuous woman must earn the trust of her husband. Verse 11 tells us that a wife is to be a refuge and a safe place for her husband. To bring this scripture into today's lingo and offer an example that drives home the point, let me say that the virtuous wife who will gain her husband's trust doesn't run from store to store charging her husband's credit card without his knowledge. She would not create a financial hardship where the husband must work two jobs just to make ends meet.

The truth of the matter is that the virtuous woman trusts God for finances, which is the key to satisfaction and happiness. As we believe God to supply our needs, the pressure is taken off of the husband or sometimes the wife to provide. Many couples disagree over finances, and studies show that financial problems are a major cause of divorce.

Unfortunately, especially in times past I've seen women put demands on their husbands to supply amply for them.

Most wives desire financial security, but the source of every good and perfect gift is our Father God. Dear women, we need to look to God as our provider. The Bible teaches us in Philippians that our God "shall supply all your need according to His riches in glory by Christ Jesus."

Let me share this. There was a time I thought that because I did nice, thoughtful little things for my husband that he was feeling my love and recognized how much I loved him. I would leave him little love notes and cook his favorite dinner. Yet, I soon learned that those gestures were tokens of love from me, but they were not speaking his language at all.

You see, men desire respect and crave reverence. God made them that way, and God goes out of His way to tell us to honor them. With this in mind, I immediately set out to respect, reverence and honor my husband, and instantly I saw a difference in the way he treated me. He responded by tenderly loving me.

In Ephesians 5 and 6 we find a survival kit for families. In these chapters, God specifically gives direction for the manner in which each family member should operate for optimum success in the home. He tells men to love their wives as Christ loves the Church and gave Himself for it (Ephesians 5:25). He tells children to honor and obey their parents (Ephesians 6:1-

3). He tells women to reverence their own husbands (Ephesians 5:33). God shares with women how to properly love their husbands and children.

Reverence is a word God uses to teach women how to love their husbands. This word means honor and respect. I have witnessed many women criticize their husbands in front of other people. I have heard women shame their husbands in front of others because they feel like they do not make enough money. I have heard women interrupt and correct their husbands while they were trying to talk. These are not honorable acts. By acting in these ways, we do not love our husbands in the way they need to be loved. God made men with the need to be respected and admired. As an act of honor to God, we should respect and honor our husbands.

If someone you highly respected was in your presence, you would not criticize, interrupt, correct, or talk over the person. Most likely, you would attentively listen to every word that came out of his or her mouth and treat the person like a VIP (very important person). God instructs us to treat our husbands in this same manner.

First Peter 3 tells us that Sara, who trusted in God (she trusted in God's ways, which are higher than our ways) obeyed

Abraham, calling him lord. Yes, that is a lower case l. Nevertheless, Sara did refer to Abraham as her lord; it was a title of respect. Jesus is our Lord and Savior, and in turn, He asks us to respect our husbands. Sara had a great respect for her husband because she trusted God.

Ephesians 6 also gives important instructions regarding our children. In my relationship with my children, I did many things for them, like washing their clothes, helping them with homework, and taking them out for ice cream. All these things are wonderful things to do for your children. But Ephesians 6 tells us that our children should obey and honor their parents, and it is the parents who must enforce these attitudes.

To obey and honor does not come automatically to a child; these behaviors must be taught. Proverbs 29:15 says the rod and reproof give wisdom; but a child left to himself brings a mother to shame. It is the discipline and instruction of a parent that gives the child wisdom.

Without a doubt this requires diligence, time, and discipline on the part of a parent to use the rod of correction and to instruct the child. However, if we do not take the time to obey God, the Bible says we will be brought to shame. Notice, it is not the sole responsibility of the father to use the rod of correction. This scripture is speaking to mothers as well.

Some mothers tell their disobedient child, "Just wait until your father gets home." Yet, the Bible instructs both parents to discipline their children.

Moreover, Proverbs 13:24 says, "He that spareth his rod hateth his son: but he that loveth him chasteneth him betimes." The word *betimes* means early, according to the Strong's Exhaustive Concordance of the Bible. You see, loving correction breeds healthy children. But Proverbs 10:13 says a rod is for the back of him that is void of understanding. Isn't it interesting that the Bible specifically mentions where parents are to correct their children – on the backside.

No wonder, God made a beautifully padded backside, where the child feels the sting of his or her disobedience. I have never understood why we do not just do what the Bible says. Through the years, I've seen parents spank children many other places – the face, the hands, the shoulders, the head. I've seen parents in stores or in public pinch their children, pull them by their hair, and grab their clothes, and I've even heard parents yell, cuss, and scream at their children. But these things ought not be so; I believe these acts are abusive and unhealthy for children.

God's instructions are simple: use a rod on the backside and instruct. It's that simple. We ought not add or take away from God's Word. If we do it His way, we will reap His rewards in our family. We are not to correct our children when we are out of control. We are not to correct them when we are angry. We are not to correct them publicly because it embarrasses them. Our motivation and intention is not to embarrass and shame them, it is to train, give instruction and bring wisdom. Our purpose is to impart understanding to the intent that our children grow up and are equipped to succeed in life.

In fact, the Bible goes so far as to say to correct your children early. That means when you are in control of yourself. That means, when they disobey or dishonor you (Ephesians 6:1- 2), correct them in a calm manner. The Bible says because foolishness is bound in the heart of a child, the rod of correction will drive it far from him (Proverbs 22:15).

In chapter 1 we read that a fool is someone who says "no God," and this is true because a fool does not acknowledge the authority of God. When foolishness is bound in a child's heart, he or she does not recognize authority. As parents we are to teach our children to recognize authority. If you do not teach your child to respect authority, others eventually will teach them. It is sad when children ultimately must be imprisoned because the police need to show them authority to correct them.

A parent once told me in great frustration that she simply could not control her three-year-old child. I found this statement interesting since I remembered visiting an aquatic park, where I witnessed dolphins perform beautifully and effortlessly from the simple commands of a trainer. So if a dolphin can obey, why would a three year old be unable to follow instructions?

The answer is found in the dedication and commitment of the trainer. Obtaining the attention of wild creatures that do not speak English and teaching them to jump when a whistle is blown, requires time, consistency, and patience. How much time, consistency, and patience do we take with our children? According to A.C. Nielsen (1998), parents spend less than **38 minutes a week** in meaningful conversation with their children. Yet, children age 2-17 watch in **excess of 20 hours** of television in a week.[3] So let me ask: Who is training the kids?

Children are not supposed to raise themselves or figure life out for themselves. Children are to be **trained**. Proverbs 22:6 says train up a child in the way he or she should go, and when the child is old he or she will not depart from it. One interesting facet from the definition of *train* means to help them develop a taste for something. By properly parenting them, you will help your children acquire a taste for God's ways.

In teaching them honor and obedience, they will begin to see the results of favor and success in their lives. We want to set them up for success. As they experience more and more success, they develop a taste for honor and obedience. They begin to taste and see that the Lord is good.

Proverbs 26:3 says, "A whip for the horse, a bridle for the ass and a rod for the fool's back." Notice that the Bible specifically speaks of *a rod* as the instrument of correction. Notice that it does not speak of a hair brush, a belt buckle, a wooden spoon from the kitchen, or a chair for time out. A rod of correction is the specific instrument used to disciple children according to God's Word.

Children should understand that they won't be corrected with anything else. Parents should not hit them with their hands. Hands are to be used for love and reassurance; touching, hugging, and holding hands with your child are signs of affection. Never strike your child with your hands, and never correct your child when you are angry.

If you have an anger problem, leave the discipline process to your spouse until you can get some therapy. James 1:20 says, "The anger of man worketh not the righteousness of God." Improper discipline harms a child, while proper discipline offers positive eternal benefits. In fact, Proverbs 23:13-14 states that positive discipline will deliver a soul from hell.

That's why Ephesians 6 instructs fathers to provoke not your children to wrath, but to bring them up in the nurture and admonition of the Lord. Wrath used against them will cause them to become angry.

Parents must not discipline their children because they are mad (the word *mad* means crazy), but rather parents should discipline their children because they love them and desire for them to live long and to live well. Ephesians 6 says that if children honor and obey, they will be well (I like to say well-off, wealthy, and healthy), and they will live a long life. This is why the Bible encourages parents to use the rod of correction.

Evil

> **She will do him good and not evil all the**
> **days of her life. Proverbs 31:12**

Let's take a closer look at the word *evil* from the text scripture above. In the Strong's Exhaustive Concordance of the Bible, *evil* is defined as giving pain, unhappiness, and misery. *Evil* also describes someone who is vicious in disposition, hurtful, and disagreeable. However, good means appropriate, pleasant, happy, kind, and ethically right. A man who finds and marries a virtuous woman clearly has an advantage in his life; their home will be a peaceful and happy place.

This may seem like a daunting task for a woman to do good all the days of her life, but it's for her benefit to adopt a lifestyle of happiness. Stress, anxiety, fear, and discontent leads to sickness, both mentally and physically. Experts say that 80 to 90 percent of disease is stress related. Women generally have more problems with depression than their male counterparts, according to one article I read.

Is it possible for us to stay happy? The Bible says, "Happy is he whose trust is in the Lord" (Proverbs 16:20). Happiness is to be derived from our intimate relationship with the Lord Jesus Christ. Our happiness does not depend completely upon our relationship with our husband and children. It is the Lord who brings stability to our emotional life. He is the joy of our salvation and the joy of the Lord is our strength. We can continually experience His joy in our lives because the Lord is always the same—yesterday, today, and forever.

When Adam and Eve fell from grace through disobedience in the Garden of Eden, certain curses fell on the woman, the man, and the serpent. In Genesis 3:16 the Lord told the woman, "…Thy desire shall be to thy husband, and he shall rule [be a tyrant in a bad sense] over thee." But today we live under a new and better covenant, and Galatians 3:13 says that those who have received Jesus Christ as Lord and Savior are redeemed from the curse of the law.

Therefore, as daughters of God, our *desire* [or longing, craving, stretching out to] should be toward God, not only our husband. Of course we are to desire, respect and adore our husbands, but we are to be most desirous of God. In other words, God is to forever maintain first place in our lives. That way, God is the ruler of our lives, and He supplies love to us and satisfies us. Then, in turn, we can be a supply of help to our husbands, instead of being a drain on them. God wants the husband to be the head of the wife and the head of the household, but God does not want the husband to be a tyrant.

We must understand and renew our minds to God's goodness and His love. Goodness is a fruit of the Spirit (Galatians 5). Love never fails (1 Corinthians 13), and therefore, God never fails because He is love (1 John 4:8). So in essence, following after love is following after God, who is omnipotent and all powerful. Any step outside of love is a step outside of God, and a step outside of His power. On the other hand, being good is very powerful. In fact, Romans 12:21 says to overcome evil with good.

Act 10:38 states, "How God anointed Jesus of Nazareth with the Holy Ghost and power, who went about doing **good** and healing all who were oppressed of the devil, for God was with Him." Matthew 5:16 says, "Let your light so shine before men, that they may see your **good** works and glorify your Father which is in heaven." Ephesians 2:10 says, "For we are His workmanship, created in Christ Jesus unto **good** works." Romans 12:21 says, "Be not overcome of evil, but overcome evil with **good**. Goodness is much more powerful than all evil."

In order to walk in God's goodness and to allow it to flow through us, we must be strongly connected to God. Actually, sometimes we do not even know how to be good. Jesus Himself said, "Why callest thou me good, there is none good, but one, God" (Matthew 19:17). Along this same line, Moses asked to see God's glory and God showed Moses His goodness. Consider that for a moment. That tells us that God's goodness is His presence, and His presence in our lives allows us to show forth His goodness. Jesus went about doing good because He was anointed by the Holy Ghost and God was with Him (Acts 10:38).

Fame and Fortune

Her husband is known in the gates, when he sitteth among the elders of the land. Proverbs 31:23

Fame and fortune sounds like the old television show, *Lifestyles of the Rich and Famous.* But do you remember what

God told Abram in the book of Genesis? He said He would bless him or empower Him to prosper and make his name great or famous. God did exactly what He promised. Abraham is still revered today as the father of our faith. Actually, it's important to God that we be influential because He desires us to impact people with His love and kindness. Young people especially need to know that God wants their lives to count and to matter. He wants to raise them up to make a difference in their generation.

This particular man in Proverbs 31 was known or recognized in the gates, which means the marketplace or public meeting or places of business activity. At the gates he talked daily with the elders or those in authority; the elders were business men and leaders of the city. In fact, in Nathanael Wolf's book, *The Gatekeepers*, he expounds on the old-walled city of Jerusalem and the city gates that were entry points. Thousands of people have passed through those gates for centuries, and that's why the gates were the perfect place for vendors for all these years. Thriving businesses are set up all along the gates, which should come as no surprise considering the important business conceptual motto: location, location, location. There are over one hundred references to the city gates in the Bible.[4]

We can gather the opinion that evidently the man's wife in Proverbs 31 had something to do with her husband being among the leaders of this community. Her support enabled him to build business relationships with other men. She allowed him to foster friendships and sit among the elite. Because this virtuous woman was secure in herself and in God, her husband was able to make a difference in that city. She was not jealous of his time spent out of the home, and she did not demand that he be with her all the time. It is good for men to have friends, and it enriches the marriage relationship.

Through the wisdom and kindness of the virtuous woman, advancement was brought to her husband. Remember the old phrase that said, "Behind every great man, there is a great woman." It's true because individuals do not become a successes by themselves. It takes the efforts of many people to bring one individual to a place of wealth and influence.

Interestingly, verse 31 tells us that this woman's works praised her in the gates. Who was in the gates talking about her works? Her husband. He was telling the elders about the diligence, love and support that his wife was to him. What can your husband say about you to his friends?

She looketh well to the ways of her household, and eateth not the bread of idleness. Proverbs 31:27

The phrase "looks well to the ways of her household" is a bit difficult to understand. I like to say it like this: the woman **looks over it, looks into it, and looks after it**. Observing and paying attention to a woman's household is a time-consuming and enormous task. However, if women will give it their full focus and pray for God's help, they will receive wisdom to correct things before they become too monumental and damaging.

'Looks Over It'

Consistent oversight of a household and recognizing the direction a family is headed, give way to course correction at the first sign of trouble. Problems usually do not happen overnight; most difficulties begin when a small problem is ignored and allowed to continue. If not confronted, problems grow more complex and difficulties can become catastrophic.

I remember flying in a private aircraft while watching the pilot respond to the air traffic controller's voice. He changed the direction on the instrument panel by turning the dial ever so slightly, which in turn corrected the whole course of the trip. This same principle applies in our lives. As parents the slightest change we make in our children's lives can bring life or death to them. By the wisdom of God, we make adjustments that keep our children on course or allow them to veer off course. Sometimes the adjustments seem simple and minor, but they still make a great impact on a child's future.

For example, I told my teenage daughter that she could not hang around with a particular girl in the neighborhood. I had never felt this way before about any of her friends, but the more I prayed about this situation, the more urgency I felt. My daughter listened to me and explained to the girl that she could no longer be friends with her. Within the next two weeks, the girl was arrested for drunk driving and in trouble with the law. My daughter thanked me for telling her to beware of this girl. God gives parents wisdom to protect their children, and we need to listen and obey the Lord as we guide their lives.

A very well-known minister told me years ago that he would invite his entire family to his house once a month. All of his children, their spouses, and his grandchildren would come and eat, and he would just look over them to make sure no devils were trying to attach themselves to his family. After all, the Bible says watch and pray. We need to watch over what God has given us.

'Looks Into It'

Women must investigate things in their children's lives. We must show an interest through getting to know their friends, teachers, principals, and even their enemies. This means getting involved in their education and in their activities. My parents were always involved in my life. In fact, any activity I took part in growing up, my parents would be right there volunteering to help.

I recall my mother serving as Brownie Scout leader, Sunday school teacher, and cheerleading sponsor. She was my fifth grade teacher and president of the PTA (parent-teacher association). My father was one of the carpool drivers for many ballet and baton classes. He was present at every gymnastics meet I competed in and coached my powder-puff football team. He also practiced tennis with me every afternoon when I tried out for the high school tennis team. Needless to say, my parents were involved. They knew everyone that influenced my life, and I could not get away with any mischief.

'Looks After It'

From time to time, your child will face opposition; unfortunately, it's a given. Maybe it will come through bullying from their peers, a difficult teacher or authority figure, or perhaps a negative encounter with a stranger. If our children are in danger or harm's way, we must be aware; we must be responsible to protect our children. Even though my parents sided with the teachers and principal if I got in trouble, I knew also that if I was unjustly treated, my parents would support and help me. They had my back. We must look after our children. They feel secure and safe when they know that we will take up for them and we are not against them.

As parents, we are not only responsible for the physical and mental well being of our children. We are responsible for their spiritual well being as well. Far too often parents rely on others, such as church leaders, to tell their children about Jesus. God ordained parents to tell their children about Jesus and to pray with them for salvation. Parents are to tell them about the baptism in the Holy Ghost and pray with them to receive. I believe the earlier mothers and fathers begin spiritual training, the better. The Bible says to teach our children when they are drawn from the breast. That is pretty young; however, they are very receptive at a young age to the Spirit of God.

As soon as my daughters began to form words, I taught them to say "I love Jesus." I prayed with them every day and told them to repeat what I said. Eventually, they began to pray without my help, and today they both know how to contact God. It is a crying shame when Christian parents do not take the time to teach their children to pray and to read the Bible. Forming these two habits of prayer and Bible reading gives children a tremendous advantage in life when they leave your house and establish their own lives. Equip them with these powerful habits and do not deprive them of the life of God.

It is not necessary to "beat them over the head" with religion; parents must gently lead children in the ways of God. I remember as a child, every night one of my parents would come in my room and read a Bible story. Then we would kneel at the foot of my bed and pray. It was a nourishing and tender time with my parent that I looked forward to every night. This practice taught me a reverence for God and a love for Jesus.

Throughout my life, I was made to go to church. Yes, I mean made to go! Even when I was in college, my parents said they would pay my tuition if I would go to church. Children do not always know what is good for them. We cannot say, "Well, when our children get older, they will decide on their own about God." What if we left brushing their teeth up to their discretion? I know my two daughters would have let their teeth turn black and fall out.

The truth is that I insisted they brush their teeth every morning and every night, and I made them take baths. So why would I be so insistent on them taking care of their physical bodies, but totally neglect their eternal spirits? How could I possibly refrain from giving them the bread of life? Spiritual life will give their mind's light and their bodies' health.

Part of equipping children with the proper, spiritual nutrition is regular attendance of a local church. Do not just drop your children off at church, attend services with them. The Bible states, "Train up a child in the way that he should go, and when he is old, he will not depart from it" (Proverbs 22:6).

In The Amplified Bible, the latter part of this verse defines the bread of idleness as gossip, discontent, and self-pity. These characteristics cause us to be idle or stuck in life. We are unable to move forward and accomplish the plan of God if we allow ourselves to wallow in discontent and self-pity. In everything we are to give thanks, for this is the will of God. Thanksgiving and praise to God will lift us out of discontent. There's also a trap set by Satan when we gossip and backbite, so the Bible warns us not to be ignorant of Satan's devices. Through yielding to idle talk, we devour one another. For where envying and strife is, there is confusion and every evil work (James 3:16).

Chapter 3

The Virtuous Woman Lives Intentionally

She riseth also while it is yet night, and giveth meat to her household and a portion to her maidens.

Proverbs 31:15

In verse 15 we continue to learn about the industrious nature of the virtuous woman who rises even before the sun to begin her day. What motivates her to work? I believe she has a clear understanding of her purpose in life. A sense of purpose fuels her vitality to get up early and start her day.

By the same token, God wants us to understand the purpose for our lives because He has a plan for each one of us as well. In fact, Ephesians 5:17 declares that we should not be unwise, but understand what the will of the Lord is. We *can know* God's will for our lives; He's not trying to hold out on us or keep His will a secret. In Ephesians 1:17 Paul prays that the "eyes of our understanding be enlightened and that we might know what is the hope of His calling."

Success and faith in life begin where the will of God is known. Therefore, it's of great benefit to take time in the Word and prayer to know God's will. Another key to discovering God's will for you is through a local church. I believe every Christian should be an active, working part of a local church. You will realize your personal vision through the vision of your local church and by the gift of the pastor as your shepherd.

Yet, taking time in the Word and prayer and attending church must be built on the foundation of a personal relationship with Jesus Christ. Above all, the first step—and the most important step—is to surrender your life to Jesus Christ. *Surrender* is a scary word, but Jesus taught that those who lose their life shall find it in Him (Mark 8:35).

In today's society many people simply exist or barely exist. They have no knowledge of the will of God or the goodness of God for their lives. They are men most miserable, like zombies getting out of bed everyday and marching off to a job they hate. After work, they march back home only to watch six hours of television they should not watch, eat things they should not eat, and drink things they should not drink. They live in an overweight, unfit, unhealthy lethargic state, not only physically, but also mentally and spiritually. This is part of Satan's strategy to paralyze God's people.

God has a better plan! Wake up and live God's plan. The Bible says to awake unto righteousness. Jesus came to give us life and give it to us more abundantly.

I believe the virtuous woman lives the abundant life with great purpose and one way she lives on purpose is to measure out portions to her maidens or employees. This word *portion* means assignments. Each morning she plans the tasks to be accomplished in her home. The Proverbs 31 woman has a vision, sets goals, and lives intentionally. She directs her day and her life—they do not direct her.

To make progress in life, a vision and purpose are necessary. Otherwise, we just stay busy, but never accomplish God's plan. God says without a vision people perish (Proverbs 29:18), so it's important for us to get a vision and to write it down. After all, God gives us an imagination, and vision is seeing what God intends for us to be. We must get His picture in our hearts of what our family should look like and how it should function. And we can do this by reading and meditating in the scriptures, by praying, and by observing people who have successful Christian homes.

Habakkuk 2:2 advises us to write the vision and make it plain, so he who reads it may run with it. To that end, ask yourself these questions. *Do I have a written vision for my home? What is God's plan for my children? Do we have goals and objectives, or do we just live from day to day and perhaps from crisis to crisis?*

Let me encourage you to assess your level of vision based on how you answer these questions via a 1-10 scale. To really locate yourself, answer each question by assigning a number of 1-10 to each of your answers. A number of one would mean you are not at all satisfied with the place where you are, and a number of 10 would mean you are completely satisfied with the place where you are. This assessment will provide you with an important point of reference.

Next you can set goals that aim you toward your target goals. Be sure your goals are clear, measureable and structured with a time limit so you can know—and be encouraged—when you've accomplished them. By knowing precisely what you want to achieve, you will also know where you have to concentrate your efforts. Properly set goals can be incredibly motivating. Otherwise, it's difficult to remain consistent in the desired direction.

Jesus shared His vision with His disciples in Mark 16:15-18. He told them to go into all the world and preach the gospel to every creature. He set the goal to get men and women saved, filled with the Holy Ghost, delivered, and healed. As you set goals, begin with the overall vision for your family. Then, break the big picture down into smaller parts. Take these goals and reduce them to everyday tasks, and incorporate these tasks until they become habits.

Then let me suggest that you review your habits from time to time to make sure you remain steady and moving toward your goals. This will take discipline for sure, but outlining your day will help you work toward the desired results. Soon, you will see your dreams become a reality.

> *She is not afraid of snow for her household:*
> *for all her household are clothed with scarlet.*
> *Proverbs 31:21*

I love the beginning of this verse. The virtuous woman is not afraid, and phrases exhorting us not to fear are used generously throughout God's Word. Instead of being afraid, God wants us to be full of faith. Our physical bodies and minds are not equipped to continually carry fear. Fear, anxiety, worry, and stress destroy our physical bodies and minds. These forces are poisonous and can be lethal. In Luke 21:26, Jesus said "men's hearts will fail because of fear."

Moreover, fear is not of God. God has not given us a spirit of fear, but of power, love and a sound mind (2 Timothy 1:7). Fear has torment, but perfect love casts out fear (1 John 4:18). Fear is the opposite of faith, and worry, stress, and anxiety are products of fear. Fear is the culprit of uncontrolled anger and pride, and it's present when people are not developed in the love of God. It is the root cause of many evils because Satan's kingdom operates by fear. Satan works through the avenues of panic, terror, alarm, dread, and fright, and we can clearly recognize that fear has torment.

On the other hand, the Bible says that we should **fear** God, but this particular use of the word *fear* means to reverence or to respect. In other words, we are to honor God. The Bible says that the fear of the Lord is the beginning of wisdom (Proverbs 9:10). Of course God does not want us to be afraid of Him. But He does desire our honor and respect so we will heed His voice and obey His Word.

Obedience is not necessarily simply for the sake of the kingdom of God, it is for our sake. For the wages of sin (disobedience) is death (spiritual separation), but the gift of God is eternal life (the Greek word for *life* is Zoë) through Jesus

Christ our Lord (Romans 6:23). Romans 2:4 tells us that it's the goodness of God that leads us to repentance. God's love and kindness draw people to Him.

Love Your Household

God is a family God, and families are important to Him. In fact, He created two institutions: the family and the church (His spiritual family), and He said in Ephesians "of whom the whole family in Heaven and earth is named." God desires to build families, and He wants them to maintain strong ties and relationships. God wants to use families in the ministry, working together in His service.

Examples in the Old Testament demonstrate God's desire to use families. Abraham was chosen to be the father of many nations because he would teach and train his children to follow God. Therefore, Abraham left a legacy of faith through his son, Isaac, his grandson, Jacob, and his great-grandson, Joseph. We need the intimacy and emotional support from our natural family and our spiritual family. You see, the devil causes division and subtraction, but God brings addition and multiplication. That is the sum total of spiritual math.

Let's team up with God. Let your family be the first and most important priority in your life. Make sure you provide support and care for your family. This is the will of God. In Ephesians 5 and 6, God gives even more specific instructions for successful families.

Husbands are to love their wives as Christ loves the Church. Wives must reverence their husbands. Children need to honor and obey their parents. Ephesians 6 makes a point of instructing fathers to bring up children in the nurture and admonition of the Lord. People assume it is solely the mother's duty to rear children, but God says that fathers are *to bring them up.*

Why is all the detailed instruction outlined in the Bible? God wants to insure strong families. Just think for a moment what would transpire if everyone took responsibility and care for his or her family according to the Word of God. How significantly transformed our modern world would be. The problems we face in today's society would diminish exponentially. Indeed, the solutions to society's problems are written in His Holy Word, and we need to apply God's principles to our households.

The virtuous woman takes her responsibilities seriously. Among many other things, she makes sure her children are clothed in scarlet. The word *scarlet* in Hebrew means "the best." So, in other words, the household of the Proverbs 31 woman is clothed with the best—not the cheapest clothes, the worst clothes, the second-hand clothes, or the hand-medowns with holes in them. No, her household is clothed with the best because God wants us to have the best.

The Bible tells us in Isaiah1:19 that if you are willing and obedient, you shall eat the good of the land. If your children are not wearing the best right now, do not be condemned. Just know that it is God's will for your family to have the best and His will allows you to operate in faith to obtain His promise of the best.

Unfortunately some women are so busy clothing themselves with beautiful garments, shoes, and jewelry, that they neglect to properly clothe their children. The kids walk around in raggedy clothes and old shoes. Yet, we see from God's Word that our children should be clothed with the best; that is God's desire and it should be a mother's as well.

Through various means, the devil deceives too many Christians into believing that his crowd should be the ones with all the wealth. The devil tries to persuade Christians to live poor, meager lives. In America rock stars, Hollywood movie stars, and athletes are idolized, and most are very rich. Their wealth is seldom questioned, but rather an accepted fact. They are admired for obtaining and possessing great riches.

However, if a man or woman of God demonstrates wealth and riches, he or she is often ridiculed, persecuted, and "drug through the mud" by the media and the public. Accusations are hurled while men and women of God are shamed for living in nice homes and driving nice cars. But the truth is that God wants His children to prosper.

God makes His will about this very clear in 3 John 2, where He inspired John to write, "Beloved, I wish above all things that thou mayest prosper and be in health, even as thy soul prospereth." We see this same precedent set throughout the Old Testament. Men and women of God were blessed by God for their obedience, faithfulness, and diligence. God provided for them richly and they possessed abundance. This provision was available to them at all times, during economic downturns, and even during times of extreme devastation. For example, Isaac sowed in the land of **famine** and received in the same year one hundred fold (Genesis 26:12). In spite of a famine or an extreme shortage of food, this covenant man prospered, and we can too.

On the other hand, we also learn from the Old Testament that when people were disobedient, unfaithful, and lazy, they came up lacking financially. In the Old Testament, if you were living in poverty, you needed to check up on your walk with God. Again, we just read that we prosper "even as our soul prospers."

The big question is why anyone would think it's holy to be poor? Where do some people get that idea? Obviously they get it from the devil, who does not want the body of Christ to have money or wealth. The devil is just smart enough to realize that the more money Christians have, the more we can accomplish for God because it takes money to preach the gospel.

There are people who think that we should not pray for money or things. Yet, Jesus Himself taught the disciples to pray for provision in the Lord's Prayer. When the disciples asked Jesus to teach them how to pray, Jesus instructed them to ask for their daily bread. "Give us this day our daily bread," He led in Matthew 6:11. I am making this point because I've heard people say, "You should not pray for things." But bread is one of the very *things* Jesus taught the disciples to pray for in the Lord's Prayer.

In Mark 11:23 and 24, Jesus says that we should believe that those *things* that we say shall come to pass. When we believe and speak, Jesus said that we shall have them. Them what? **Them things.** I realize that is not proper grammar, but this helps us understand that we must pray for provision. Many Christians live far below what God has provided for them financially because they do not pray for finances. The Bible says we have not because we ask not (James 4:2). The bottom line is that God is our source and supply in life; we must not look to the hand of man, but to the hand of God.

I've heard religious people say, "Well, God is not into things." I beg to differ. God made all things, and He *is* into things. Haggai 2:8 states, "All the silver is mine and the gold is mine, saith the Lord of hosts." The earth is the Lord's and the fullness (the entire contents) thereof (Psalms 24:1). In 1 Timothy 6 the Bible states, "That we should trust in the living God, who giveth us richly all things to enjoy." Not only is God into things, but God is also into richly giving all things to His children.

Interestingly, in our society drug dealers have a reputation of being rich and driving fancy cars, and we wonder why young people get drawn in to selling drugs. Some young people think this is the only way they will ever accumulate a lot of money. Religion has lied to our youth and told them that if they serve God, they will never have anything. But this way of thinking is contrary to the Bible and is designed to keep Christians poor and keep young people out of the ministry.

My parents owned and operated a motel in Panama City Beach, Florida, while I was growing up. Money was tight when we first built the motel, but as time progressed the business became very prosperous. When I was 20, the Lord spoke to me about His call on my life and directed me to go to Bible school. I was sharing this with one of my parent's friends, and she replied, "Oh my, Scarlett, you're going into the ministry?

I am so sorry for you, because you are accustomed to having the finer things in life."

Her comment startled me. She was not the least bit excited about my future in the ministry, but instead she was horrified that I had chosen the ministry. Her lack of knowledge of the goodness of God led her to believe that I would live a life of poverty and lack. How regrettable that we discourage young people from serving God because of the impression given through ignorance that God will not bless them. God says in Psalm 35:27 that He hath pleasure in the prosperity of His servants, not the poverty of His servants. He especially wants His ministers' blessed.

I have heard Christians say, "Stay away from money because it's the root of all evil." But they misquote 1 Timothy 6:10. The Bible says that "**the love** of money is the root of all evil." Loving money is where people get into trouble; having a love relationship with money *is* the root of evil. The Bible says to love the Lord your God with all your heart, with all your strength, and with all your soul (Luke 10:27). Obedience to this scripture leaves no place in our life to love money.

Money is just a tool. Sure, God wants you abundantly blessed, but He also wants you to bless others. God wants His children to have plenty of money because Christians should be the ones sponsoring the preaching of the gospel throughout the earth. After all, Proverbs 3:10 says our barns shall be filled with plenty, when we honor God with our substance. Joel 2:26 states, "...ye shall eat in plenty." God is a God of plenty, and it's His desire for us to be women of plenty. Remember, one definition of *virtuous* means wealthy.

On the other hand, the Bible states that money will ruin a fool. So, don't be a fool—be wise. Wisdom brings blessings to our lives, and as we prosper, we will flourish, not be ruined by money.

There's another significant idea and a powerful, spiritual principle expressed in Proverbs 31:21 where it describes the household of the virtuous woman clothed with scarlet. The phrase *clothed in scarlet* ties to the scarlet thread of redemption outlined in the Bible from Genesis to Revelation. This scarlet thread of redemption points us to the powerful blood of Jesus Christ that was shed for all mankind.

Consider this. The virtuous woman is not afraid for her children because they are clothed in precious blood. The blood was put over the door posts at Passover so that the destroyer could not enter into the house. Her children were covered in the blood, so that the destroyer had to pass over them.

If we're in the family of God, we can appropriate this blessing for our children as well. After all, God says our children shall be mighty upon the earth (Psalms 112:2).

Women Preachers?

Since Psalms 35:27 speaks of God's servants, I would like to address the age-old question of women in ministry. I believe we must weigh all the scriptures and scrutinize the statements twisted through religious teaching. Too often falsehoods keep women from serving God in the capacity to which God has called them, so we have a responsibility to rightly divide the word of truth (2 Timothy 2:15).

First and foremost, we must not be ignorant of Satan's devices. After all, Satan hates women. He hates the church, and his plan is to diminish the number of laborers in the fields of harvest at every opportunity. The smaller the group of harvesters, the smaller the harvest, and the result is fewer people hear the good news of the gospel. Jesus said the harvest is plenteous, but the laborers are few (Matthew 9:37).

Let's begin by exploring this topic of women in ministry, which stirs much controversy in the religious world. Let's examine 1 Corinthians 14:34 in detail. "Let your women keep **silence** in the churches; for it is not permitted unto them to speak, but they are commanded to be under obedience, as also saith the law."

Notice the word used here is *silence*, not silent. *Silence* makes reference to an environment conducive to learning. People have to be able to hear in order for them to learn. We were taught this principle in kindergarten; basically, do not talk while the teacher is talking.

The exhortation made to these women is to be quiet while others are teaching. It says to **keep the silence.** It does not say **to be silent.** Even in modern times, women are known for their many words, and in fact, history tells us that this had become a problem in the early church. Women were talking during church.[5]

Notice also that this scripture refers to a law, but what law? Is this a law of God or the law of man? We cannot find any such law in the Old Testament or the New Testament, so this law is a custom of man.

Look at a similar scripture in 1Timothy 2:11 where it says, "Let the woman learn in silence with all subjection." Particularly notice that this scripture does not say let the woman be silent. Rather it says let her **learn in silence.** When you think about it, how else can one learn? In other words, one must be quiet and listen in order to learn.

The next verse states, "But I suffer not a woman to teach, nor usurp authority over **the man,** but to be in silence. For

Adam was first formed, then Eve." Think about this. The scripture is referring to husband and wife or to Adam and Eve. It's not dictating behavior for all women.

The scripture does not specify that women in general not teach. No, it's saying that wives should not usurp authority over their husbands. Notice also that the Bible refers to "**the man**," not all men. Therefore, women are not subject to all men, just to their own husbands (Ephesians 5). A wise woman realizes that she cannot teach her husband anything anyway; God shares this truth with us. A wise woman is to **respect** her husband and **teach** her children.

Understand that *usurp* means to seize and hold office, place, or power by force or without right. The definition further means to seize or exercise authority or possession wrongfully, according to the Merriam-Webster On-line Dictionary. No doubt, God set order and authority in the family, and Ephesians 5 tells us that the husband is the head of the wife. However, that does not mean that all men are the head of all women, which is a most important differentiation.

First Corinthians 11: 5 goes on to say that "every woman that prayeth or prophesieth with her head uncovered dishonoureth her head." Who is her head? Her husband. So again, women should be under the spiritual authority of their husbands. There is safety under spiritual authority. Why? Because the angels are able to help and protect us according to 1 Corinthians 11:10.

Does this mean that women are less important or less significant than men? Of course not. This has to do with God's order in the family and roles that He gives each one in the family to help the family unit function properly. These directives, when carried out as God instructs, assure the success and strength of the family.

Clearly, God's intention is not to devalue women, but to advance and raise women to a new level in Him.

Bible Accounts of Women Speaking in Church

Let's look further into God's Word for examples concerning women preachers. First let's look at the example of the prophetess Anna in Luke 2:36-38. Though she was a widow of great age, the Bible says that she did not depart from the temple, but served God with fastings and prayers there night and day. Notice in verse 38, "She **coming in** [to the temple] that instant gave thanks likewise unto the Lord, and **spake** of him [in the temple] to all them....

We read here that Anna spoke in the temple. Well then, was she out of order or out of God's will because she spoke aloud in church? Did they try and stop her? Did they picket outside the temple with signs saying women ought to be silent? Of course not. Notice here also that men and women were present in the temple listening to her speak because the Bible does not say that she spoke only to women. No, Anna ministered right there in the temple to both men and women.

Quite honestly, the Church is generally very hypocritical toward women. Some churches will not allow women to teach during services, but they promote special music every service in which a female sings a song. That's ironic when you think about it because songs deliver powerful messages. Actually, singing is teaching in the strictest sense of the word.

In fact, the Bible encourages in Colossians 3:16 that Christians should be **teaching** and admonishing one another in songs and hymns and spiritual songs. So, therefore, if it is against the rules for women to teach in church, we should not let women sing in church. To keep silent means to keep silent. But the truth is that these church leaders do not really believe the mandate of women being quiet anyway because they allow women to teach through songs.

A second area of hypocrisy found in certain religious circles is a refusal to allow women to teach in American churches while many of these same circles totally support women sent as missionaries to live and teach and pastor in overseas churches. There's certainly no Bible mandate that says women cannot teach in American churches, but they can teach elsewhere in the world. Would scripture give different rules for different countries? Why would it be okay for women to teach overseas, but not here in the United States of America? If it's truly wrong here, then wouldn't it be wrong there?

A third hypocrisy is found in the area of teaching Sunday school classes. In many church circles where women are not allowed to teach in church, the women are still allowed to teach Sunday school classes. But is Sunday school not in church? How then can women teach in Sunday school? How is it acceptable for women to teach men in Sunday school? Is there an age limit set for a boy when he can no longer be taught by a woman? Is it 12, 18, or 25? Is this not all foolish and ridiculous? The Bible does not say that a woman cannot speak in church and cannot teach boys or men. Indeed the entire body of Christ needs to rightly discern the Word of God.

Here's another Bible example to consider. Phillip had four daughters all of whom prophesied in Acts 21:8-9. To whom did they prophesy? The answer is to the church. How can that be if it were really true that women could not speak in church? After all, according to 1 Corinthians 14 to prophesy means to edify the church. So if women were not to speak in the church, then why would the Holy Spirit empower them to prophesy to the church? Of course He would not go against God's will.

In fact, Acts 2 states that in these last days, "God will pour out of His spirit upon all flesh and your sons and your **daughters** shall prophesy and your servants and your **hand-maidens** shall prophesy." Did God not know that women were not supposed to speak in church? How silly for so many Christian churches to be so confused and misinformed when God's Word is so clear on the topic.

Consider another Bible example of women in ministry. In Matthew 28:7 we find the angel of the Lord commissioning two women to go quickly and **tell men** (Jesus' disciples) that Jesus was raised from the dead. Therefore, two women were the first preachers of the good news of our risen Savior and Lord. This should kick over some sacred cows.

Furthermore, throughout the New Testament, we find women holding ministry positions listed in Ephesians 5. Junia, a Roman woman converted before Paul, was spoken of by Paul in Romans 16:7 when he praised her as being outstanding among apostles. Priscilla, listed before her husband in the ministry team, evangelized with Paul in Ephesus. In Acts 18:18-26, Priscilla and Aquila taught the very learned Apollos.

Priscilla and Aquila in Romans 16:3-5 established a church in Rome and risked their lives for Paul. Euodia and Syntyche, two women in Philippians 4:2 and 3, evangelized with Paul publicly[5].

The list continues. In Romans 16:1-12, Phebe was a **diakonon** of the church in Cenchrea. The same Greek word translated *servant* here is translated *minister* in 22 other scriptures[5]. Another example is found in Colossians 1:25, which says, "I was made a minister according to the stewardship from God bestowed on me for your benefit that I might fully carry out the preaching of the Word of God" (NAS).

Phoebe was most likely the pastor of this church in Cenchrea. Paul said of her in verse 2 that she was a **succourer**, which means a female guardian, protectress, patroness, caring for the affairs of others and aiding them with her resources. She was a wealthy female, able to travel and deliver the book of Romans 800 miles from Cenchrea, near Corinth to Rome. She supported many works and Paul's ministry as well[5].

Many other women held positions of leadership in house churches. Lydia had a church meeting in her home in Acts 16:14-15 and 40. Chloe, who had converts from her church group, was mentioned in 1 Corinthians 1:11. Nympha in Colossians 4:15 is the only leader mentioned by name in her town house church. Stephanas in 1 Corinthians 16:15-16 is said to have been devoted for ministry to the saints. Paul urges the members to be subject and subordinate themselves to her household, indicating that he is indeed talking of ministers with authority[5].

Then in 2 Timothy 1:5, Paul speaks of Lois and Eunice who greatly influenced the young Pastor Timothy. Paul said that he remembers the unfeigned faith in Timothy that was first in his grandmother and his mother. One note of interest is that there is no mention of Timothy's father or grandfather. His success in ministry was due to the two women in his life, and both *taught* him faith and instilled in him what they had learned of God. Notice that Lois and Eunice were not rebuked by Paul for teaching a man; instead they were honored.

I've often wondered if it's wrong for a woman to teach a man, why would God name two books of the Bible after women such as Esther and Ruth? Esther and Ruth were mighty women of God, whom He honored and spoke freely of in the Word. Esther was actually a Moses-like leader, who delivered and saved a whole race of people from annihilation. Risking her own life, she unveiled the wicked plan of Haman to King Ahasuerus. Through the wisdom God and through her willingness to obey Him, Haman was hung on the gallows designed to kill Mordecai.

It's astounding to me that God used a little orphan girl named Esther to rescue an entire nation. Though she was raised by her cousin Mordecai, God raised her up from a lowly position to that of royalty. Esther's end was much brighter than her beginning—so much so that she ended up with much more wealth after her courageous stand for the Jews. In fact, the house of Haman and his riches were awarded to Esther and Mordecai after his death.

Similarly, we might go through some hard times, but if we stay steady and obey God, we will be more blessed after the storm passes. God wants to raise us up the same way He raised up Esther.

Women in Leadership Positions

Another woman of power we read about in the Bible is Deborah. In Judges 4 we read of this married woman who is a prophetess and the judge of Israel. One day she for calls Barak and speaks to him by the Spirit of the Lord. She tells him that God hath said to gather together ten thousand men and go to war against King Jabin's army of multitudes in Canaan.

Deborah tells Barak the outcome of the war. She says, "God will give them into your hand." In verse 8 Barak makes the most interesting request. He asks Deborah to go with him to war. He even says if she will not go, neither will he. Think about that for a minute. Don't you wonder why a man would plead for a woman to go to battle with him? He actually refused to go if she did not accompany him.

My opinion is that he understood the power of God on Deborah's life, and he understood that she was a virtuous woman. Her strength and power were so evident that he desired the presence of God on her to be with him during battle. She was so courageous that without hesitation she agreed to accompany him to the battlefield. However, she did continue to say that the journey would not be of honor to him because Sisera, the general under Jabin, would be slain by a woman.

Barak did defeat the nine hundred chariots of Sisera's army and killed every soldier, except Sisera. He fled the scene and came upon the tent of a woman named Jael. She invited him in and when he fell asleep, she took the nail from her tent and hammered it into his temple, killing him. Just as Deborah had foretold, Barak was victorious and General Sisera was taken out by a woman.

Obviously, God uses women in battle.

And God wants to use *you* in His warfare. We know our warfare is not natural, but spiritual and mighty through God to the pulling down of strongholds.

Chapter 4

A Virtuous Woman: Entrepreneur

She seeketh wool and flax and worketh willingly with her hands. Proverbs 31:13

We are all the recipients of unique gifts and talents from God. First Corinthians 12 and Ephesians 6 outline the many different parts of the body of Christ. Even in the natural realm, everyone is gifted with something in particular. Some women, like the virtuous woman, enjoy making garments from wool and linen. Others are creative entrepreneurs. Some are skilled airline pilots, teachers, doctors, lawyers, artists and the list goes on and on.

Actually, I think we are most miserable when we do not create and produce. Each of us needs to recognize the gifts with which we are endowed and be faithful to develop these gifts by working willingly with our hands. God promises as we separate ourselves from wrong influences, delight in His law, and meditate therein night and day, whatsoever we do will prosper (Psalms 1:1-3).

However, God also requires that we **do** something before He prospers us. Deuteronomy 8:18 states that God gives us the power to get wealth that He may establish His covenant in the earth. One translation substitutes the word *produce* for *get*. In other words, He helps us produce, not just get handouts.

Productivity is vital to a woman's life. Being productive adds energy and vigor to our existence. The Proverbs 31 woman gathered materials and produced garments. With a remarkable passion, willingness, and a splendid attitude, she created with her hands through God's power. Indeed God made mankind to produce; His desire is for us to bear fruit.

For instance, an apple tree is fruitful when it **produces** apples. John 15:8 tells us the same principle applies to Christians when it says, "Herein is my Father glorified, that you bear much fruit." God gives us the power to produce (get) wealth, and God is not just talking to men; He's talking all mankind.

Jesus taught how important it is for men and women to produce in the parable of the talents (Matthew 25:15). Three men were given certain amounts of money, and they were expected to increase these finances. The first two men doubled their money, but the third one, the one who had been given the least amount, was **afraid** and hid his master's money. He was reprimanded for this, and his master called him slothful, wicked, and lazy.

Unfortunately for him, fear was not an excuse that was accepted by his master. It's also not an acceptable excuse for us in the use of our talents. Mark 11 instructs us to have faith in God because God expects us to act in faith and then produce. He wants us to increase, and He expects us to make a profit.

God unfolds two central ideas for our success: faith and work. Embrace both of these virtues, and you will be abundantly blessed. Even though work is a four letter word, it is not a curse word; work is healthy for us. The Bible says in Proverbs 6:6, "Go to the ant, thy sluggard (lazy), **consider her** ways and be wise." As we consider the ways of the virtuous woman, the Bible makes it clear that she also worked. She did not sit around all day watching soap operas or talking to her friends on the phone. With God's empowerment coupled with her willingness to work, she was able to produce great wealth.

In modern times there is a controversy over whether or not women should work outside the home, and yet the Bible offers many examples of women who worked outside the home. One of the first scriptures that comes to mind is Titus 2:5, which declares that women should be **keepers at home**. The Amplified Bible says women should be **homemakers**. What do these phrase mean? Does it mean that women should only keep the home?

Certainly God knows that our homes ought to be kept and be a haven for our families, a refuge from the cares of the world. They ought to be clean, neat, and properly furnished, and this responsibility is laid at the feet of the woman. However, this does not mean women cannot leave the house. Being at home all day long everyday does not necessarily make you a homemaker. I know some women who are at home all day and their houses are a complete mess.

This reference to women being "keepers at home" simply means that the woman should oversee the household duties, which she can accomplish through supervising and delegating responsibilities. The virtuous woman of Proverbs 31 did not do all the work herself; she had help. In the New Testament we find women like Dorcus, Lydia, and Priscilla, all of whom worked willingly with their hands in other professions outside the home.

In Acts 9:36-42 we read the story of Dorcus, called Tabitha, who lived in the city of Joppa. The Bible says she was full of good works and almsdeeds or giving to the poor.

Verse 26 says, "And it came to pass in those days, that she was sick and died: whom when they had washed, they laid her in an upper chamber."

The disciples sent two men to tell Peter to come quickly and not delay, so Peter hurried to go with them. Verse 39 says, "When he was come, they brought him into the upper chamber: and all the widows stood by him weeping, and shewing the coats and garments which Dorcas made, while she was with them."

But verse 40 says that Peter "put them all forth" or sent them out of the room or outside. "...He kneeled down and prayed; and turning him to the body said, Tabitha, arise. And she opened her eyes: and when she saw Peter, she sat up." Verse 41-42 continues, saying, "And he gave her his hand, and lifted her up; and when he had called the saints and widows, presented her alive. And it was known throughout all Joppa; and many believed in the Lord."

The people around Dorcus adored her and refused to accept her death. They told Peter how she had done good works and made garments for them, and as Peter prayed the power of God raised her from the dead. I was amazed as I pondered the great strides her friends took to revive her. I began to wonder if I were to die suddenly if people would take time and intercede to God on my behalf to extend my life. Or would those around me not be burdened by my passing? Would those around me possibly even be glad I was gone?

We need to ask ourselves these questions, and we need to examine our lives and see if we are ministering and caring for others. Are we helping people? Are we a blessing or are we burdening others? For certain God desires for us to bless others. How we live and how we treat others matters very much to God. And it matters to others as well because Dorcus's community loved her so much, they went out of their way to find Peter and convince him to pray for a miracle.

In the book of Acts, we read of another woman who worked in the garment industry. Acts 16:14 tells us that her name was Lydia, and she was a seller of purple. We could put it this way. Lydia sold high-end garments from her own business that rivaled today's Sax Fifth Avenue or Niemen Marcus.

We know this was true because purple was a color worn by the elite. We see an example of this in Luke 16:19 in the life of the rich man who talked with the beggar, Lazarus. He was clothed in purple and fine linen and fared sumptuously every day. You'll also recall that Proverbs 31:22 described the virtuous woman as wearing silk and purple, again emphasizing the wealth she possessed.

Evidently Lydia's business thrived. The Bible says she owned quite a large home because she invited Jesus and all of His disciples to stay with her. Even during the time that Paul and Silas were thrown into prison, the other disciples were staying in her home. Here is a New Testament woman, high-lighted in the book of Acts as a successful businesswoman and a prayer warrior. God opened her heart, and she prayed everyday down by the riverside. Lydia was a woman of wealth spiritually and financially.

She layeth her hands to the spindle, and her hands hold the distaff. Proverbs 31:19

Second Thessalonians 3:10 tells us that if a person does not work, the person should not eat. God Himself works, and in fact, the entire Trinity works—Father, Son, and Holy Spirit. Throughout the Bible, God worked mighty works. Jesus said, "I must be about my Father's business" (Luke 2:9). The Holy Spirit is at work in us both to will and to do of His good pleasure (Philippians 2:13). So God expects nothing less than work from His children.

Certainly the verses in Proverbs 31 demonstrate the diligent nature of this highly successful female. Being reared in the south, I would describe the virtuous woman this way: "There is not a lazy bone in her body."

On the other side of the coin, mankind is given to extremes, and we must watch ourselves to remain balanced in life. Though work and labor are required by God, we should not **toil**. Actually, there is a significant distinction between toiling and laboring, and we must beware because there are ditches on either side of the road. If we're not careful to remain in the middle of the road, we can easily fall into a ditch on one side or the other. Matthew 7:14 says the way is narrow that leads to life.

The word *toil* is a verb used in the book of Genesis after the fall of Adam and Eve. God told Adam in Genesis 2 that because of sin the ground would be cursed. In Genesis 5:29 Lamech, Noah's father, mentioned the toil of his hands due to the ground being cursed. *Toil* means to grow worrisome, painful, or sorrowful[1].

Then in the New Testament, Jesus tells us not to toil in Luke 12:27. He said the lilies toil not, and observe how beautiful God has clothed them. He goes on to instruct us to seek first the kingdom and His righteousness and all these things shall be added unto you. It is God's good pleasure to give you the kingdom.

As Christians the Bible instructs us to labor in prayers, in good deeds, in the fields of harvest, and in the Word. James 1:25 states that we are to be a doer of the work. Ephesians 4:38 says that men should labor, working with their hands. Clearly, we are told to work, but not to toil.

Peter in Luke 5:1, on the lake of Gennesaret, told Jesus that they had toiled all night and had taken no fish. Jesus told them to let down their net. Work is necessary, but in the life of a Christian, there should be no toil. Jesus relieves us from carrying heavy burdens that lead to exhaustion and weariness. The Bible says those that wait (serve) upon the Lord shall renew their strength. The Lord maketh rich and addeth no sorrow to it (Proverbs 10:22).

As Peter and his partners let down their nets, they were astonished at the draught of fish they caught. There were so many fish that their nets were breaking. Of course, they were overjoyed, because this heavy a load of fish was the equivalent of a substantial payday. This was their livelihood, and God suddenly increased their income tremendously. God blessed their skill.

The virtuous woman also had skill and knew how to work with textiles. She was proficient, and God was able to bless her expertise. God desires to bless our skills as well. I particularly try to encourage young people to develop skills and invest in themselves and improve their abilities. We might not necessarily be enrolled in an educational institution, but we should always continue to learn. Cultivate a love for reading and be open to take in new information to sharpen skills.

Reading, for instance, is vital to our Christian walk. In 1 Timothy 4:13, the Bible states, "Till I come, give attendance to reading, to exhortation, to doctrine." Our culture is inundated with television, movies, and video games. Televisions are now placed in most restaurants and in stores, and Neilson research states that the average American watches T.V. 28 hours per week. But the Bible says the important thing is for us to show ourselves approved unto God, **workmen**—and women—who need not to be ashamed, rightly dividing the word of truth (2 Timothy 2:15).

Training is essential. Too many times, we expect to be promoted without acquiring new skills. Discover how to excel in what you are called to do in life. Find someone who has done what you want to do and gain knowledge from them. Paul said, in what you have both learned and received and heard and seen in me, do (Philippians 4:9). He set an example for others to follow. To learn from others, we must humble ourselves. As we grow, we will also be an example for others to follow.

The New Testament instructs us to be followers. Most people desire to be leaders, but the only reference to leadership in the New Testament, surprisingly, is the blind leading the blind; they both fall into the ditch (Matthew 15:14). Yet, absolutely, God calls us to be followers of Him. Moreover, God wants us to be skilled laborers and discover the thrill of developing new skills. It is even important to the health of your brain to learn new things and to do new things. No matter what your age, continue to be a student.

> *She maketh herself coverings of tapestry: her clothing is silk and purple. Proverbs 31:22*

God records two seemingly, unimportant ideas. Yet, I believe this verse showcases a beautiful balance in the life of the virtuous woman. She made herself something fine, **and** she also tended to the needs of others. First she met her own needs, and then she looked after the needs of others.

As a minister for over 30 years, I have encountered many women with low self-esteem. They are consumed with the needs of others and trying to solve or meet those needs, regardless of how it affects their own physical, mental, emotional, or spiritual life. Some women have come close to death because of the toil it takes on their mind and body. Yet, God did not call us to meet the needs of everyone around us. He is the need meeter.

Psalm 23 says, "The Lord is my shepherd, I shall not want (be in need)." He is the source and supply. As grandmothers, mothers, wives, and daughters, we must not take on the role of the Holy Spirit. We are not the Holy Spirit. Then what is our role in other's lives? Our role is one of prayer and obedience. God will perfect and perform the work needed in someone else's life. Jesus said that we are to love our neighbor as our self. But if we do not love ourselves, we are unable to love others.

Someone may say, "I'm not worth loving." But that person would be forgetting something important—to remember whose we are and who we are in Christ Jesus (in union with Him). God loves each of us with an everlasting love. He feels we are worth loving, so we are worth loving. Our heavenly Father thought highly enough of us to send His only begotten Son to pay the price so we could spend an eternity with Him. God feels we are worth the precious and most costly blood of Jesus that was shed for us. We **are** valuable and precious to God.

John, one of Jesus' disciples, had tremendous revelation of God's love for him personally. Again and again in the Bible

John refers to himself as the beloved of God. John 19:26 says, "When Jesus therefore saw his mother, and the disciple standing by, whom he loved." John 20:2 says, "The other disciple, whom Jesus loved." John 21: 7 says, "That disciple, whom Jesus loved." John 21:20 says, "Seeing the disciple, whom Jesus loved following…."

John 13:23 says, "Now there was leaning on Jesus' bosom, one of His disciples, whom Jesus loved." John was assured of Jesus' love for Him, not just for others. That love kept him. At one point, his enemies could not even kill him. Historians recorded that they tried to boil him in oil. They eventually just exiled him to the Isle of Patmos, where he then continued his close relationship with His loving Lord and wrote the book of Revelation.

We need to build our faith in God's love for us like John did. We do this by reading and mediating on the love scriptures, but also by confessing daily that He loves us. We must speak of His great love for us personally and remember ***God loves women.***

The virtuous woman of Proverbs 31 made tapestries or spreads or coverlets for herself and took time to beautify her home. Just a side note here, but I think it's worth mentioning. Our bedrooms should be kept clean, beautiful, and comfortable. We spend one-third of our life sleeping. Rest prepares us to handle all the responsibilities of life and helps us enables us to accomplish our tasks and goals. If our mattress is uncomfortable or our pillows are old and worn out, we cannot get the proper rest we need. If our bedroom is cluttered, messy, or filthy, it will affect our mind and emotions. We will have a hard time getting to sleep.

We usually spend more money on the other rooms in our homes, probably because we think more people see these rooms. However, we should place a high priority on our bedrooms and invest in the room where we spend a lot of our time. We need nice furniture, curtains, and proper lighting. We should take time to find a proper mattress and pillows. Making your bedroom an environment of beauty and rest will bring tranquility to you. If you're married, you and your spouse will look forward to bedtime, and it will aid in peaceful sleep. If you're single, your bedroom will be your personal oasis and place of private solace.

Attired in Purple

Not only did the virtuous woman make fine linen of purple, but she also wore purple. This is significant. Why? I believe reference is made in Proverbs 31 to the color of her clothes because the color purple signifies wealth.

The virtuous woman is not a poverty stricken little woman who wears frumpy clothes; she wore the best. She took care of herself and clothed herself with the finest attire available. Some religious minds would accuse her of not being spiritual. In some religious circles, one is looked down upon if he or she wears nice clothes, has nice hair styles, or wears expensive jewelry. Religious folks sometimes quote 1 Peter 3, which says that the behavior of women should not be that outward adorning of plaiting the hair, and of wearing gold, or of putting on of apparel; but the hidden man of the heart.

Yet, I asked the Lord about that very scripture. I said "Lord, is it wrong to wear nice clothes, have gold rings, and fix my hair?" He answered by saying several things to me. He said His desire is for me is to live from my heart—from the inward man, not the outward man.

He also stressed to me that I should always be brighter on the inside than I am on the outside. Think about that for a minute. He explained that He did not mind if I sparkled and shined with jewelry, but the emphasis of my life must be endeavoring to continually be filled with His brightness (His love, character, humility, joy, and strength).

Truly the most important aspect of our physical lives on earth is to let God sparkle and shine through us as Christian women. Jesus says, "Let your light so shine before men that they may see your good works and glorify your Father which is in heaven" (Matthew 5:16).

If God was against wearing jewelry, we would not see Bible examples of godly men and women exchanging rings. For instance, if God was against jewelry, He would not give rings to those who overcome as described in the book of Revelation. We have another Bible example in Genesis 24 when Abraham's servant went to find Isaac a wife. Verse 22 says the servant took as a gift "a golden earring of half a shekel weight, and two bracelets of ten shekels weight of gold." So obviously the Bible does not forbid jewelry.

We are God's ambassadors and represent the most high God, and we must look good to show forth His glory. We are children of the King, a royal priesthood. God takes pleasure in our prosperity, and He is not ashamed when we prosper. We are to have everything that heaven has, and heaven is not a poor place.

The Lord Himself instructed us to pray, "Thy will be done on earth, as it is in heaven." No one in heaven is poor, lacking, hungry, homeless, dirty, or behind in his or her bills. In heaven the streets are made of gold and the gates are made of one pearl (Revelation 21:21). The walls of the city are made of jasper (Revelation 21:18). Many other precious stones are named as building material in heaven including emeralds, sapphires, and amethysts. It surely doesn't sound like our heavenly Father is poor or lacking financially.

We need to renew our minds to how much God loves His children and to the wealth of God He has prepared for us. He is the best Father that can be found, and He wants the best for us. He said if there are parents who are evil who we being evil know how to give good gifts to our children, how much more shall our heavenly Father give good gifts to them that ask Him (Matthew 7:11).

Chapter 5

A Virtuous Woman:
CEO and Landowner

She considers a field and buyeth it, with the fruit of her hands she planteth a vineyard. Proverbs 31:16

The Spirit of God spoke to me one time and asked, "Do you know why many women do not own their own property?"

Then He answered, saying, "The reason is because they have never even considered it."

His statement really caught my attention, and it's interesting to ponder. Here, however, we have the virtuous woman who did think about it. She looked at a field, envisioned it, counted the costs, considered the benefits, and ultimately purchased it.

Unfortunately, too many times I think we as women do not step out in faith to even consider what we can do.

God wants us to think big.

God wants us to dream.

God is a "can do" God, and He said you can do all things through Christ who strengthens you (Philippians 4:13).

Let me encourage you to look in to your heart and get in touch with the desires of your heart. What has God put in your heart? Recognize those things and then consider them because God has given them to you. Meditate. Gather information. And pray.

Mary Kay Ash, founder of Mary Kay Cosmetics, is quoted as offering important advice that can benefit us all. She has said, "If you think you can, you can. If you think you can't, you're right."[6] Begin to imagine doing what God has put in your heart. Then, just take a small step toward fulfilling your dream. An ancient Chinese Proverb says: "The longest journey begins with the first step." Do not despise the days of small beginnings.

The virtuous woman had confidence and courage to buy property. The financial transaction was her choice, and Proverbs 31 does not mention her husband having anything to do with the purchase. She considered it, and she bought it. Praise God!

We also must be courageous and obey the Lord in matters of finance. God told Joshua to be strong and courageous, and successful people are people who are full of courage. Generally, this has been an area where men have flourished while too many women have allowed inferiority to rule their lives. They are content with living far below the financial level God intends for them. But it is high time for women to be strong and courageous. God wants us to succeed. He wants us to thrive financially.

When God made or cut covenant with Abraham, He said, "I will make you the father of many nations." He said I will bless you and make your name great (Genesis 12:2). You shall be a blessing, God said, as He changed Abram's name to Abraham.

But notice something important. God did not simply cut covenant with Abraham. God didn't tell Abraham, "By the way, your wife, Sarai, is covered under the agreement I made with you. Let her know, will you?" No, God went to Sarai and talked to her just as He had done with Abraham. God promised He would bless her and bless her body (Genesis 17:16). He also changed her name from Sarai to Sarah, and in 1 Peter 3 God referred to all of us as her daughters.

You see, the Bible doesn't just talk about Father Abraham, but also about Mother Sarah. A name change signifies that a covenant was established between God and all mankind—men and women. For that very reason, God's mighty covenant of prosperity is for women as well as men.

In Galatians 3 the Bible says that Christ became a curse for us, that the blessing of Abraham might come on the Gentiles. He said that in Christ there is neither Jew nor Gentile, bond nor free, **male nor female.** We are all in Christ, and we are all **heirs** according to the promise. Women who know that they have a covenant of prosperity can activate the covenant themselves and step right on over into a place of abundance.

I've been concerned for years about women's finances. Research from The National Poverty Center at the University of Michigan indicates that poverty rates are highest for families headed by single women. Some 28.7% of households headed by single women are below the poverty line, while 13.8% of households headed by single men are poor, and 5.5 % of households headed by couples are poor.[7]

Single women struggle financially, especially when they have children. Yet, at the same time, God takes special interest in single moms. In two different instances, we see the prophets Elijah and Elisha ministering to single mothers. In the book of 1 Kings 17:9, God sent Elijah to the brook during the famine and fed him. The brook dried up, and the Lord told him to go down to Zidon where a widow would sustain him. He probably thought, *Wow, God is sending me to a rich widow to feed me during this drought.*

Surprisingly, when he arrived and asked for food, this single mom said she only had enough for herself and her son. She had only enough for one meal before they would die. Elijah gave her some pretty startling advice. "Give it to me and do not be afraid."

God sent Elijah to a lady who was basically broke and gave her an opportunity to activate the law of sowing and reaping. Essentially the prophet told the woman who was broke and starving to sow into the anointing and reap a miracle. When she did, God provided enough for the woman, her son, and Elijah to eat for an entire year. Now that is abundant and supernatural provision.

In 2 Kings 4:1, Elisha ministered to a woman with two boys, whose husband had died. She was unable to pay the debt, so the creditor was coming to take her children and make them slaves. Notice that Elisha offered her help by asking an unusual question.

"What's in your house?" he asked.

"Nothing," she quickly replied. But suddenly she remembered one thing she had in her possession.

"I have a little bit of oil in a jar," she explained. That's all that was needed.

We must remember that seeds are small, but inside them is the ability to produce a large harvest. If a seed is sown, it will bring forth. Elisha put this woman in the oil business. He instructed her to borrow vessels and to pour out the oil. The oil multiplied, and she poured until all the vessels she had borrowed were full. Elisha told her to go sell the oil and pay the debt and for her and her sons to live off the rest.

We may think at times that we do not have anything, but we always have seed to sow. We know this is true because 2 Corinthians 9:10 says God gives seed to the sower and bread for food. No matter our circumstances, we do have seed in our possession. We must become aware of what we have, instead of focusing on what we do not have.

God always works with what we possess. This principle of being conscious of what we have right now in our hands is a key to being successfully in God's system of finances. When Jesus fed the multitudes in Matthew 6:41, He did not just call bread down from heaven. No, He asked His disciples what was available among the crowd of people.

A little boy had only his lunch of five loaves and two fish, which was brought to Jesus as seed. Jesus took the small lunch and looked up to heaven, blessed it, and then fed at least five thousand people.

We know the virtuous woman was familiar with sowing and reaping because scripture says with her own hands she planted. The woman believed in planting, and the Bible assures us in Psalm 1:3 that whatsoever we do will prosper. So she put her hands to something and that something prospered. But keep in mind that we must do something before it can prosper; we must plant before we can reap. We cannot sit around and do nothing and expect to prosper.

Does that mean that we'll all be millionaires? Well, when you think about it, a million dollars frequently is not enough to get the job done. But the Bible says we will have all sufficiency in all things that we may abound to **every good work** (2 Corinthians 9:8). I know a lot of good works, don't you? We must believe God for abundant wealth in order to sow to every good work.

To be wealthy means that all the resources of heaven are available to you. Women, you have a covenant with God. This covenant of prosperity means that everything that God has is yours, but it also means that everything you have is God's. Your covenant assures us that you can ask God for *anything* He has, and He can ask for *anything* you have. Wow—what a covenant through Jesus Christ.

Many people don't realize that a covenant includes exchange. Some people want everything God has, but they are not willing to give God what He requests from their resources.

Some people even refuse to pay the tithe or a tenth of all of their increase, much less allow God access to anything else they possess.

But the truth is, if we desire to walk in supernatural prosperity, we must recognize His Lordship over everything we have in our possession. Ultimately what we have is not ours anyway. The Bible says the earth is the Lord's and the fullness thereof. The silver and the gold are God's (Haggai 2:8). The property and possessions we have do not really belong to us; we are simply God's stewards or managers. Therefore, if we're not faithful with what He puts into our hands, we can lose it.

The Bible says that a steward must be found faithful (1 Corinthians 4:2). It is a requirement. Financial blessing comes only when we acknowledge He is the source of our blessing. Financial blessing and abundance come as we totally surrender and obey what God says to do regarding our finances, and this explains why so many Christians are poor.

You see, not all Christians have entered into covenant agreement with God in the financial realm. God has offered to covenant with every Christian, but not all have accepted. Greed, fear, or ignorance keeps them ensnared and living way below their covenant rights of wealth.

Nevertheless, God has made a way through His Son Jesus for every man and woman to live in abundance, and it's

God's desire that we are blessed with more than enough in every area of life. He will turn our "not enough" into more than enough if we only follow His instructions. The Bible says if we are willing and obedient, we shall eat the good of the land (Isaiah 1:19).

In 2 Corinthians 8:9 the Bible says, that though "… Jesus was rich, yet for your sakes He became poor, that ye through His poverty might be rich (increased with material goods, abundantly supplied)." When did He become poor? When He was born? No, He was born into a covenant family, a family of wealth. Mary and Joseph were not poor; they had money. Joseph was not a poor cabinet maker; he was a wealthy architect and contractor that some think built the most beautiful waterfront neighborhoods of Nazareth on the Sea of Galilee. Jesus was rich in His earthly walk.

Even in His adult life in ministry, Jesus walked in covenant rights. After all, He had a treasurer and not too many poor people have treasurers to hold their few coins. The Bible also points out that Jesus owned His own home (John1:39). In fact, Jesus said in Mark 14:7, "The poor you will have with you always, but not Me." Notice that He made a distinction between Himself and the poor; He did not classify Himself among the poor.

Some might say, "But Jesus was poor. He was even born in a manager." But it's not because Jesus was poor that He was born in a manager; He was born in a manager because the hotel was full. Actually, when Jesus was born, money started hunting him down. The wise men came and opened up their treasures to Him and even financed His trip to Egypt where Jesus' family fled at the instruction of God to escape Herod's wrath.

During His ministry, twelve disciples and later seventy more disciples depended upon Jesus for their livelihood. He had a huge and very successful ministry, and the Bible says that Jesus continually gave to the poor. How can you continually give to the poor if you are broke yourself?

"Then why did He borrow a tomb," someone asks. Jesus did not borrow a tomb because He was poor, but because He only needed it three days. In fact, His clothes were so valuable that the Roman soldiers gambled for them.

The truth is that Jesus was not poor at all; He was rich. The Bible says that Jesus became poor on the cross. At the same time He bore our sin, Jesus bore our sicknesses and our poverty once and for all. He became sin so that we might be saved. He became sick, so that we might be healed. And He became poor, so that we might be made rich.

He did all this on Calvary for you and for me – for every man **and woman**. Praise His holy name! To not accept what

He bought and paid for on the cross would be to spit in His face. If we do not walk in all that He provided for us, we are saying that we do not care that He redeemed us and paid the price for us with His own life. It's through our actions and our words that we tell Him if we are grateful for what He has provided for us.

I've heard people say, "I don't need or want to be rich." They think they are being selfless, and yet, they are really being quite selfish. In essence what they're really saying is that if they have just enough for themselves and their family they will be quite happy.

Pastoring for more than 30 years, I've heard other people say, "Oh, pastor, I do not need all this prosperity stuff. I really do not need any more money. I have enough for my family. We have a home, a car, a boat and a lake house." What a self-centered, uncaring, self-absorbed person! Does that person think that because he or she has enough that's all that's needed?

What about helping others? What about the poor? What about supporting the gospel? This life should not be just about us. This covenant is about a lost and dying world, and we must believe God for abundance to give abundantly. We need to finance the end-time harvest that must be brought in before Jesus returns. God wants you blessed, so you can be a blessing.

God told Abram in Genesis 12:2, "I will make of thee a great nation, and I will bless thee, and make thy name great; and thou shalt be a blessing." Jesus bought and paid for our financial well being in His redemptive work on Calvary (2 Corinthians 8:9), and we need to release our faith for all the resources available to us through His sacrifice. We don't believe this way just so we can have all things richly (1 Timothy 6:17) to enjoy, but so we are able to abound to every good work. Deuteronomy 8:18 tells us that He gives us the power to get wealth to establish His covenant in the earth.

Let me offer this example. A friend of mine owns a farm, and he goes to great expense to plant, water, and harvest his crops. Why does he spend so much money? Because he knows during harvest season, he will reap a great deal of money—much more than he has invested. God will likewise abundantly bless those who sow and work in the fields of His harvest, which are the souls of men and women.

Actually, women have a special place in financing the gospel. This precedent is stated in Luke 8:1-3 where the Bible tells us that Jesus went throughout every city and village, preaching and showing the glad tidings of the kingdom of God. Verses 2-3 tell us, "Certain women, which had been healed of evil spirits and infirmities, Mary called Magdalene, out of whom went seven devils, and Joanna the wife of Chuza Herod's steward, and Susanna, and **many others**, which ministered unto Him of their substance."

They contributed out of their own resources to support the ministry of Jesus and His disciples. These women financed the ministry of Jesus. Often, we think only men are financiers, but here in the in the New Testament, we find **many women** financing the gospel. I believe that today God wants to use women to finance His gospel around the world.

Will we accept the challenge? Will we enter into covenant relationship with Him? Are we as daughters of the Most High God willing to believe and receive the wealth that He has laid up for the just? Will we be obedient to give whatever He says to give? Will we believe God for a return on our financial sowing—some 30-, 60-, 100-fold—in order to continually increase our giving?

The harvest is already white unto harvest, but how can the world hear the gospel unless a preacher is sent or sponsored? It takes money to preach the gospel so rise up women of God and receive your inheritance to sponsor the preaching of the gospel.

She perceived her merchandise is good; her candle goeth not out by night. Proverbs 31:18

The virtuous woman of Proverbs 31 is all about quality control. She inspects her merchandise and refuses to let things slip by her. Excellence is her way of life, and even if long hours are required to do a project well, the virtuous woman stays up late to get the job done.

Quite simply, a good work ethic will procure a good job. My father taught me that when I worked as an employee, I should arrive at work early every day—never be **just** on time. He would tell me to be there early and stay past quitting time, even if it's just five minutes. What is ten minutes a day to you? But that time spent at work communicates loudly to your boss that you are diligent, caring, and committed.

My father also taught me that while you are at work, find something to do even if you've finished your assigned task. Do not just stand around the water cooler and talk, and do not sit at your desk and play video games. Help someone else, come up with new ideas, get ahead on your own work, or simply pick up a broom and sweep. Don't be idle. I can assure you that you'll be greatly rewarded for your efforts.

I practiced these habits through the years, and I've been promoted at every place I've worked. I've also never been fired. When I was working my way through college serving in a restaurant, I was asked to be a manager. When I was doing my internship for my master's degree, the agencies where I worked begged me to work for them. Was it because I was so talented or smart? No, it was my work ethic that got their attention.

The Bible says in Luke 16:12 that we must be faithful in another man's vision before we will receive our own vision. God said if you will be faithful in a very little, He will give you more authority (Luke 19:17). If you are taking care of what you have right now, then God will increase you. Unfortunately, this explains why so many people are at an impasse at their present place of employment and not increasing financially. Some people just perform the minimum amount of labor to barely get by during their work hours.

In Daniel 1:20 we read that Daniel, Meshach, Shadrach, and Abednego were found to be ten times better than any other of the king's men. The Bible said they had an excellent spirit (Daniel 5:12), and this spirit of excellence caused Daniel to be preferred among all other "employees." It also caused these men to be promoted time and time again after many taxing tests and trials. Through the reign of three kings, Daniel and his friends not only miraculously survived death sentences, but also prospered and became mighty and influential.

In this same manner, God empowers us for excellent work. Yield to that spirit of excellence, and you will become ten times better than those around you who have no covenant with Almighty God.

> **She maketh fine linen, and selleth it: and delivereth girdles unto the merchant. Proverbs 31:24**

Thank God for girdles. He will give you creative ideas for products that will be high in demand among the population. God knew we needed girdles and this woman manufactured them. In fact, she was involved in every facet of business. She was in production, marketing, sales, and distribution, and I believe there is an important parallel for us today. God is concerned about every area of our life—not simply spiritual areas.

God will anoint us in every area of our lives. He will empower you to do your secular job just as He empowered the virtuous woman to do hers. The Proverbs 31 woman was powerful in business, and you can be also. Remember to draw off of God's power and wisdom in your daily tasks, and you will not be disappointed.

Chapter 6

A Virtuous Woman: Physically Fit

She girdeth her loins with strength, and strengtheneth her arms. Proverbs 31:17

As women of God, we have a responsibility to take care of our physical bodies. We were fearfully and wonderfully made by the Lord, and our bodies are not our own. We have been bought with a price. In fact, the Bible tells us in 1 Corinthians 6:19 that our bodies are the temple of the Holy Ghost.

So just as we take care of our church buildings, we must take care of our temples of flesh. We maintain, clean, beautify and make sure our brick and mortar churches are excellent for the Lord's work, and likewise our body temples must also be kept in a superb way.

Consider 1 Timothy 4:8 that says, "For bodily exercise profiteth little: but godliness is profitable unto all things." The Amplified Bible expounds on the verse by saying, "For physical training is of some value (useful for a little), but godliness (spiritual training) is useful and of value in everything and in every way, for it holds promise for the present life and also for the life which is to come."

This scripture is not saying don't exercise at all because it's a waste of time. On the contrary, the scripture actually encourages us to exercise physically for the present time and to exercise spiritually for the present time and the future time to come.

I'm a certified fitness instructor, and I've taught exercise classes for women for more than 25 years. So let me assure you that it's never too late to start an exercise program. Studies have even been conducted with the elderly in nursing homes, and researches have found that even light, simple, movement helps people feel better, become more mobile, and build strength, and improve quality of life.

Our bodies need exercise—at least some form of daily exercise to condition our bodies. After all, the virtuous woman strengthened her loins, which would be the area of her lower back. Proverbs 31 says she also strengthened her arms. I choose to believe that she was diligent to work out at the gym, the walking park, or the equivalent of her day. I choose to believe that the virtuous woman worked out with her friends or her fitness trainer.

Always check with your doctor before beginning an exercise program. But keep in mind that fitness experts recommend at least 30 minutes or more of aerobic exercise three to five times a week to maintain cardiovascular fitness. Strength training is important to maintain muscular fitness and is recommended at least twice a week. One must also consider exercise to preserve flexibility and balance, and stretching is essential for our bodies to maintain elasticity.[8]

She is like the merchant's ships, she bringeth her food from afar. Proverbs 31:14

We also read that the virtuous woman travels about to obtain food. The verse says she brings it from afar; she was not a lady of convenience. She went out of her way to find good food. As we maintain our households, it behooves us to take time to find healthy and nutritious food for our families. Fast foods and convenience foods are often packed with empty calories, hidden fat, and sugar. God expects us to feed our families with fuel that will facilitate health and energy to their bodies and minds.

Caring for our physical bodies is essential because our bodies are also our earth suits. If we destroy it, we are unable to fulfill our destiny. As we look back at history, one finds that most people suffered and often died from diseases like pneumonia and tuberculosis. In recent times, people often suffer and sometimes die from self-inflicted diseases.

The leading cause of death in America is heart disease, often caused by poor diet practices, overeating, stress, and lack of exercise.[9] Luke 21:34 says, "Take heed to yourselves, lest at any time your hearts be overcharged with surfeiting and drunkenness and the cares of this life and (so) that day come upon you unawares."

Continually eating processed food that contains very little nutrition, if any, is a definite risk factor to shortening one's life span. The virtuous woman did take precautions to feed her family properly. For sure the right way to do something is not necessarily the easiest or least expensive. Sometimes it takes much more time and diligence to do the right thing, the right way.

The route of least resistance can lead to destruction. Nutritious food may be more costly in the short term, but overtime feeding your body safe, vitamin-packed foods contributes to health. This saves you a tremendous amount of money from doctor's visits, expensive prescription drugs, and exorbitant medical bills.

Obesity among American children has risen from 6% among 6-18 year olds in the late 1970s, to 15% in 2000 and the numbers are still climbing. These children are at high risk of cardiovascular diseases such as high blood pressure, high cholesterol levels and type II diabetes[5]. Statistics tell us that one out of three women in the United States is considered obese, which means a body mass index of 30 or higher for these women.[9]

The devil comes to steal, kill, and destroy—and he wants to destroy mankind. There's no question that obesity is destructive. It is at epidemic proportions in America. Even more to the point, gluttony is a sin. Many Christians wink at overeating, but condemn those who have other addictions. But the Bible says we must judge ourselves lest we be judged. Actually, the Bible says if you are given to appetite, put a knife to your throat. This is a strong and blunt way of saying: put a stop to overeating (Proverbs 23:2).

You are a spirit, you have a soul (mind, will, and emotions), and you live in a body (1 Thessalonians 5:23). God intends for you to nourish and develop your body, mind, and spirit. Compare your being to a refrigerator. In order for it to work properly and preserve what is on the inside, the refrigerator's three-pronged plug must fit properly into an electrical outlet. If all three prongs are not properly connected to the power, everything in the refrigerator spoils. You also are a three-pronged being. You must plug all three prongs—spirit, soul, and body—into a healthy, godly lifestyle in order to properly preserve everything on the inside of you.

Furthermore, what you eat and serve at home will affect your children's eating habits. Children mirror what their parent's do. Like it or not, the way we eat makes an imprint on our children; parent lifestyles are a guidebook. So we must beware of what we're eating and begin to make changes if we're eating unwisely. This will automatically bring a healthier style of diet to our children.

Proverbs 23:21 says, "For the drunkard and the glutton shall come to poverty: and drowsiness shall clothe a man with rags." Lavishing ourselves with food and drink causes sluggishness, and this unhealthy, low-energy lifestyle affects our financial status. God wants His daughters to feel alive and full of energy, which means bringing our eating habits into submission to Him.

Chapter 7

A Virtuous Woman: Philanthropist

She stretcheth out her hand to the poor; yea, she reacheth forth her hands to the needy.

Proverbs 31:20

In 2 Timothy 3:1 the Bible tells us that in the last days perilous times shall come. It does not say, "Behold, there shall be terrorism and nuclear bombs." But it does tell us in verse 2 that the dangerous times shall come because men shall be **lovers of their own selves**, covetous, boasters, proud, blasphemers, disobedient to parents, unthankful, unholy, without natural affection, trucebreakers, false accusers, incontinent (no self-control), fierce, despisers of those who are good, traitors, heady, high minded, and lovers of pleasures more than lovers of God. Seemingly there is no end to the pitfalls of self-ishness, and yet, God's plan is that we live far from selfishness.

God has a much better plan for our lives.

People are sometimes frightened by the idea of surren-dering their lives to the Lord, but what God desires for us is to have life and have it more abundantly. Some think if they serve God they will never have any fun. How odd.

The truth is found in Psalm 16:11, which says, "Show me the path of life; in thy presence is fullness of joy; at thy right hand there are pleasures for evermore." There are all kinds of pleasures in walk-ing the path of God's will for your life. The first step is to surrender from selfishness. In verse 20 of our text Proverbs 31, we read that the virtuous woman was definitely not self-consumed. Notice how she reached out and stretched herself forth to others, setting aside time to minister to others.

Unfortunately too many people are so consumed with their own lives that they miss God's intent to work through them to help others. Isaiah 58:6 asks, "Is this not the fast I have chosen? To loose the bands of wickedness, to undo heavy burdens, and to let the oppressed go free, and that ye break every yoke? Is it not to deal thy bread to the hungry, and that thy bring the poor that are cast out to thy house? When thou seest the naked, thou cover him, and thy hide not thyself from thine own flesh? Then shall thy light break forth as the morning and thine health shall spring forth speedily and thy righteousness shall go before thee; and the glory of the Lord shall be thou rereward" (NKJV).

The virtuous woman reached out to the poor and needy from her wealth, but she herself was not poor or needy. Obviously it is hard to reach out to the poor and needy when you are the poor and needy. How are you going to pay someone's electrical bill if you cannot pay your own bill?

Jesus ministered to the outcast and continually gave to the poor. In John 13:27, when Jesus told Judas to go do what he had to do, the disciples thought that Jesus was telling Judas to go give to the poor. Why? They expected it because it was an integral part of the ministry of Jesus. The disciples were accustomed to Jesus giving to the poor.

Proverbs 19:17 says, "He that hath pity upon the poor, lendeth to the Lord; and that which he hath given will he pay him again." You see, God is very attentive to your giving. He said He keeps up with it, and He will repay. We should not expect the poor to pay us back, but God will repay us.

Jesus paid particular attention to the offering in Mark 12:41. He sat over against the treasury and beheld how the people cast money into the treasury. He noticed that many who were rich cast in much. Obviously Jesus noticed how they gave and how much they gave. After all, the Bible calls Jesus the High Priest over our tithe, so even today He is very aware of your giving and mine.

Some people do not think it is important to Jesus if they tithe or how they tithe. Yet, according to God's Word, Jesus knows and cares very much. Not only did He watch people give, but also He addressed it publicly. In Mark 12:41-44 Jesus told the crowd that the poor widow woman had given more than all of them. Jesus pointed out that even though the amount she gave was small, the percentage of what she gave was huge. She gave all she had to the Lord. Jesus said something similar in Luke 6:38, which says, "Give and it shall be given unto you."

As women we need to be in covenant relationship with God financially. Some of the poorest people in America are women, but God has a solution. He wants us to hook up with Him financially through tithes and offerings. Why? Because Malachi 3 says that if we will bring our tithes and offerings to the storehouse or the local church, that God will open the windows of heaven in our behalf. What will happen? God will pour us out a blessing or empowerment there's not room enough to receive. That is quite a blessing!

Matthew 6:33 says, "If we will seek first the kingdom of God [God's way of doing things financially] and His righteousness all these things shall be added unto us." What things is this verse talking about? The preceding verses refer to clothes, food, houses, and the riches of Solomon.

Make no mistake that Solomon was among the richest man who ever lived. The Bible says that the queen of Sheba visited Solomon to see for herself of his great wealth, and she fainted because of the immense prosperity she witnessed. No doubt Solomon possessed an amazing fortune if the sight of his property and belongings brought a wealthy queen to her knees. She was royalty, yet she was astounded by such riches.

Was Solomon's wealth a result of asking God for money? No. The Bible tells us that Solomon asked God for wisdom. What is wisdom? It is knowing how to do things God's way, and when we do things God's way, we are blessed. God's way brings a full supply and all the resources of heaven.

Kathryn Kuhlman said in her book *Daughter of Destiny* that wisdom is seeing things like God sees them, looking through God's eyes.[10] Help us, Lord, to walk in Your wisdom.

Let us each purpose to make sure we lead a life of giving, and in return God will make sure we are fully supplied. God's Word says in 2 Corinthians 9:6, "He which soweth sparingly shall reap also sparingly; and he which soweth bountifully shall reap also bountifully." So who determines our harvest? Not God. We determine our harvest by the amount we sow.

Too many people think that our harvest is all up to God, but that's just not Bible. The Bible makes it clear in Galatians 6:7 that "Whatsoever a man soweth, that shall he also reap." If your harvest is small, check up on your giving. Just like a farmer cannot reap a crop where he has sown no seed, we cannot expect a financial harvest if we have not sown financially.

So many Christians pray for finances, but they do not sow for harvest. God's system is always seed time and harvest. Therefore, if what I have financially is not enough for what I need, I know that money is seed. Seeds are sometimes small, but they can produce great fruit.

Giving and receiving is God's system of economics just like breathing is God's system to sustain life. As a matter of fact, we cannot just keep breathing in or we'll die, and we cannot just keep breathing out or we'll die. There is a rhythm to properly maintain life. And in order to experience success in finances, we must also give and receive. Of course faith is required to give and receive, but that's ok because our God works by faith.

Chapter 8

A Virtuous Woman: Inner Qualities

> **Strength and honor are her clothing: and she shall rejoice in the time come. Proverbs 31:25**

The description of the virtuous woman found in verse 25 begins to discuss this model woman's inner qualities, and we begin to understand that her strength was an important part of who she was. Actually, strength should be an important part of who we are as well.[10]

Let's take a closer look at the topic of strength and begin by understanding how strength is renewed in our lives. God's Word tells us that those who wait upon the Lord shall renew their strength (Isaiah 40:31). But keep in mind that the definition of *waiting* does not mean to sit in the lazy boy recliner and anticipate what might happen next. *Waiting* means serving. A waitress serves people in a restaurant, continually watching her customer's table to make sure they have everything they need. Those who wait on the Lord serve Him, and thereby receive strength that carries them in life.

Actually, this principle of attentively waiting and dutifully serving explains why many Christians are weak. Too many Christians sit idle and allow 20% of the church people to do 80% of the work and service to God. Yet, we just saw from the Word that if people will serve and work, they will be filled with strength.

Ephesians 6 says, "Be strong in the Lord and in the power of His might." In other words, our strength comes from the Lord. The virtuous woman takes this realization one step further and keeps herself covered in it; strength is her clothing. Frequently, when we think about strength, we think about masculinity. But the Bible exhorts women to be strong—not in an offensive way, but in a godly way. The Bible makes it clear that men and women are to walk in the power of the name of Jesus.

The virtuous woman is also clothed with honor, which is definitely a missing component in today's society. We used to have the honor code, the honor roll, and the honor society, all revolving around honor. But where is honor today? It used to be that if you were to question the validity of someone's statement, you might ask, "On your honor?" In those days, a person would not dare to lie because his or her honor was at stake, and honor was a most precious commodity back then.

But in today's world we compensate for a lack of honor with lie detector tests, drug tests, background checks, I.D. checks, security checks, and sworn and notarized affidavits. That's only the short list. It is amazing how much dishonor costs a society.

The word *honor* means to be heavy or weighty (Strong's Exhaustive Concordance of the Bible[1]). Therefore, when we give honor to a person, he or she carries great weight and importance in our lives. His or her words are weighty. In 1 Samuel 2:30 God says those that honor Him will He honor. God's Word is above man's word because it carries much more weight, and we honor God by obeying His Word.

In the Bible we are told to honor God and people, so let's look at whom we are to honor. Deuteronomy 5:16 and Ephesians 6:2 state we are to honor our father and our mother, that it may be **well** with us, that we may live long on the earth. Honoring our parents brings wholeness, physical wellness, mental wellness, and financial wellness.

First Timothy 5:3 says to honor "widows who are widows indeed." First Timothy 6:1 says to honor your masters or we would say "employers." First Peter 2:17 says to honor the king, and First Peter 3:7 exhorts husbands to honor their wives. Romans 12:10 says that we ought to honor one another. First Thessalonians 4:4 says to honor our vessel, which means to respect our own bodies. First Timothy 5:17 says that those who labor in the Word and in doctrine are worthy of **double** honor, which means the five-fold ministry gifts are to be honored twice as much as anyone else. We know from Ephesians 4 that these ministry gifts include the apostle, prophet, evangelist, pastor, and teacher.

Proverbs 4:7 states that wisdom will bring you to honor. Solomon asked God for wisdom and knowledge in 2 Chronicles 1:10 to judge the people. He honored others through this request and put their welfare before his own.

What happened because Solomon was honorable in prayer? God spoke to him and said, "Because thou hast not asked riches, wealth or honor, nor the life of thine enemies, neither yet hast asked long life, wisdom and knowledge is granted, and I will give thee riches, and wealth, and honor, such as none of the kings have had that have been before thee, neither shall there any after thee have the like" (2 Chronicles 1:11 AMP).

Jesus came to restore honor to mankind, and we can read throughout the New Testament how He restored honor to several women. In Luke 13:11 we find a woman who had a spirit of infirmity eighteen years, and was bowed or completely and permanently bent over. The Bible said she could "in no wise lift up herself."

Imagine the shame that that evil spirit had brought into her life for all those years. She had walked bent over, unable to look at people, unable to walk with her head up. Jesus saw her and called her to Him, saying, "Woman, thou art loosed from thy infirmity." He laid His hands on her and immediately she was made straight and stood up glorifying God! As she was made straight; health and honor were restored to her.

Another woman in Luke 8:44 came behind Jesus and touched the border of His garment; immediately the issue of blood or hemorrhaging she had experienced for 12 years ceased. His power restored her body and made her whole. Jesus said to her, "Go in peace." He restored her health and restored honor back to her life.

In John 8:1-10 the scribes and Pharisees brought an adulterous woman and set her in the middle of the court. They said to Jesus, "Master, this woman was taken in adultery, in the very act." What shame and dishonor they brought to her. Right in the midst of temple, they accused her.

Jesus answered them in verse 7 by saying, "He that is without sin among you, let him first cast a stone at her." When they heard this, they were convicted by their own conscience and went out one by one. Jesus was left alone with the woman standing in the center of the court. He said unto her, "Woman where are those thine accusers? Hath no man condemned thee?"

"No man," She said.

"Neither do I condemn thee: go, and sin no more," Jesus said as He restored this woman to honor.

At Jacob's well Jesus sat down, wearied from His journey. A woman of Samaria came, and He asked her for water. She was astonished that a Jew would ask a woman of Samaria for a drink because the Jews had nothing to do with the Samaritans. Although she had been married five times and was now living with a man, Jesus talked with her about living water. He told her that if she drank of this water, she would never thirst again. She partook and her life was changed forever. She proclaimed that He was the Christ to all the people of that city. He restored honor to her and made her a minister, and many believed on Him because of her testimony.

Proverbs 15:33 says, "The fear of the Lord is the instruction of wisdom and before honor is humility." Our responsibility is to humble ourselves in the sight of God, and He will lift us up. He will give us honor, for honor comes only from God.

Proverbs 11:6 states, "A gracious woman retaineth honour." The virtuous woman rejoices in the time to come. She does not dread the future because her trust is in the Lord; she eagerly anticipates tomorrow with joy and delight.

> *She openeth her mouth with wisdom; and in her tongue is the law of kindness. Proverbs 31:26*

Besides being clothed with strength and honor, we read here that the virtuous woman understands the importance of her words. That's a lesson many of us could learn. After all, Proverbs 18:19 says, "Death and life are in the power of the tongue: and they that love it shall eat the fruit thereof."

You see, God is a god of words. He spoke everything into existence in the book of Genesis. He said "light be" and there was light. In Mark 11 Jesus instructs us to use the same principles; Jesus instructs us to talk to things. Verse 23 says, "For verily I say unto you, That whosoever shall **say** unto this mountain, be thou removed and be cast into the sea, and shall not doubt in his heart, but shall believe that those things which he **saith** shall come to pass, he shall have whatsoever he **saith**." This principle worked for the virtuous woman; when she opened her mouth, wisdom flowed out.

One of my favorite scriptures is in Psalms 19:14, "Let the words of my mouth and the meditation of my heart be acceptable in they sight, Oh Lord, my strength and my redeemer." This verse carries such an important message because there are times all of us need to speak certain words that are the will of God for us, our children, and our husbands. Other times, we must put a guard over our mouths. Just because we think something, does not mean we should say it. Proverbs 21:23 states, "Whoso keepeth his mouth and his tongue, keepeth his soul from troubles."

First Peter 3:10 states, "For he that will love life and see good days, let him refrain his tongue…." James compares our tongue to that of the bridle in a horse's mouth and the rudder of a great ship. Our mouths guide and direct our lives. I heard a minister make this simple but profound statement years ago: The sovereignty of God is in your mouth.

Unquestionably, wisdom is the principal thing (Proverbs 4:7), therefore in all your getting, get understanding. How do we get wisdom? James 1:5 says, "If any of you lack wisdom, let Him ask of God, that giveth to all men liberally and upbraideth not; and it shall be given him." You can count on wisdom to know what to do in any situation. In Ephesians 1:17 Paul prayed a prayer for the spirit of wisdom, and it's a prayer you also should pray for yourself.

Law of Kindness

In the Bible we find many spiritual laws. For example, there is the law of faith (Romans 3:27), the law of the spirit of life in Christ Jesus (Romans 8:2), the law of sin and death (Romans 8:2), and the royal law of love (James 2:8). And here's one more to add to the list. In Proverbs 31:26 the Word speaks of the law of kindness.

A law is a law because it works every time you work it, and kindness is a powerful law. God's Word says we can overcome evil with good. In fact, kindness is a fruit of the Spirit, and it safeguards us from harm. In Ephesians 4:32 the Bible says to "be kind one to another, tenderhearted, forgiving one another, even as God for Christ sake hath forgiven you."

Chapter 9

A Virtuous Woman: Excels

Many daughters have done virtuously (well), but thou excellest them all. Proverbs 31:29

What a statement! This woman far excels any other woman previously mentioned and listed in the Old Testament. She runs the race that is set before her and wins the prize. She achieves first place among the most prestigious women of faith, some of which include Sarah, a woman blessed of God and the mother of nations (Genesis 17:16); Miriam, the prophetess who took a timbrel and led the Israelite women in praise to God (Exodus 15:20); Deborah, the patriotic military advisor (Judges 4:4-10); Ruth, the woman of constancy (Ruth 1:16); Hannah, the ideal mother (1 Samuel 1:20, 2:19);

the Shunammite, a most hospitable woman (2 Kings 22:14); and above all Queen Esther, (Esther 4:16) the woman who risked sacrificing her life for her people. That's quite a list and still the virtuous woman excelled above them all.

The Word declares that the virtuous woman in Proverbs 31, who loved her family, prospered in her businesses, served her community, and took care of herself, far surpassed women who did great feats for God. How could this be?

I believe the fact that God chose the Proverbs 31 woman as a model woman—above every other noteworthy woman of the Bible—demonstrates just how much God observes what we do every day all day long. He watches how we handle our lives; He watches how we handle others; He watches our hearts. The virtuous woman was not a media icon, she did not do great feats for God, and she never knew great fame from man. Nevertheless, God said she "excellest them all" because her daily—seemingly average life—was very important and very powerful in the eyes of God; He approved of how she lived her life.

So why was the name of this model woman never actually written down in the Bible? I believe one reason why is so that you and I can put our names in Proverbs 31 and become the virtuous woman.

Favour is deceitful and beauty is vain, but a woman that feareth the Lord, she shall be praised. Proverbs 31:30

I was reading an article years ago about a research project conducted to find out what attracted men to women. Through interviewing men, the researchers questioned them about the characteristics of women that seemed most likely to catch a man. What would captivate men more than anything else— was it beauty, youth, personality, or something else? Interestingly enough, researchers found a common thread among the men's answers.

It did not seem to matter to the men about a woman's appearance, her age, whether or not she had been divorced, or even whether or not she had children. What seemed to be the most significant factor to attract the opposite sex was the level of confidence the woman possessed. Confident women scored the highest in attracting men.

I like to think of it this way. Faith is another word for confidence, and faith in God will make you attractive. There's no question in my mind that the reverential fear of the Lord will make you desirable.

How can this be? We find the answer to this question and the foundation of the life of the virtuous woman in Proverbs 31:30, "Favour is deceitful and beauty is vain, but a woman that feareth the Lord, she shall be praised." We must understand and walk in the fear of the Lord if we desire to attain the same level of power that radiated from the life of the virtuous woman.

Let's consider what the fear of the Lord is and is not. Most importantly, the fear of the Lord is not being afraid of God. We know this because the Bible says that God has not given us the spirit of fear, but of power, of love, and a sound mind (1 Timothy 1:7). The fear of the Lord is a respect and a reverence for Him, His Holy Spirit, and His Word. This means He is the final authority in our lives, that we are totally surrendered to Him.

Living in a reverential fear of the Lord means we do not walk in our own ways, but in His ways. For example, God tells us in His Word to forgive others. To fear Him would mean that we forgive. We choose to forgive not because we feel like forgiving, but because He told us to do so; we obey Him because His Word is the final authority in our lives. Remember, Jesus and His words are one. The scriptures in John declare that the Word was made flesh and dwelt among us. Therefore, Jesus is the Word, so for us to fear the Lord, we must fear His Word.

The fear of the Lord is the beginning of wisdom (Psalms 111:10). The fear of the Lord is the beginning of knowledge (Proverbs 1:7). The fear of the Lord is to hate evil (Proverbs 8:13). The fear of the Lord prolongs days (Proverbs10:27).

The fear of the Lord is strong confidence (Proverbs 14:26). The fear of the Lord is a fountain of life (Proverbs 14: 27). By humility and the fear of the Lord are riches and honor and life (Proverbs 22:4).

We must build this foundation of total trust in God before any other relationship in our lives can be truly established and stable. God must be our unshakeable foundation, and we must be rooted and grounded in Him. Once this connection is made, He raises us up to do things that far exceed our imaginations. Things we never thought we could accomplish, we become able to do. Draw upon Him and be filled with living water.

The theme of the whole chapter of Proverbs 31 is found in this verse. The woman was virtuous because of her reverent and worshipful fear of the Lord. Indeed Proverbs 9:10 says that the fear of the Lord is the beginning of all wisdom. This is the true foundation of her life, and she is valued by God.

In 2 Peter 1:5 we find a list seven virtues that we are instructed to add to our lives. It should not surprise us that all of these virtues are present in the life of the virtuous woman: faith, knowledge, temperance, patience, godliness, brotherly kindness, and charity. More to the point, verse 8 says if these are in you, you will be fruitful in the knowledge of Christ. You will flourish and abound.

We must respect God, His Son Jesus, His Spirit, His Word, His ministers, His children, His Church, His Plans, and His purposes to reach the world. As we do this, He enables and empowers us to achieve levels of success that are completely impossible for man—or woman—alone, but very possible through God.

Chapter 10

A Virtuous Woman: Receives Benefits

> *Her children arise up, and call her blessed; her husband also, he praiseth her. Proverbs 31:28*

I believe we should pay close attention to what our children and our spouses are saying about us. Even though this can be scary, it is vital information to acquire. Are they calling us a blessing or a burden? Are they singing our praises or slandering us behind our backs? Of course not all decisions we as parents make are popular with our children. Yet, generally speaking, our spouses and our children should be happy and satisfied.

Before I received a revelation of the powerful woman of Proverbs 31, I somehow imagined this woman lying on her death bed. Her little children came in the room to tell her goodbye, and they said, "Mom, you were such a blessing." Then her husband came in the room and thanked her for all her love and hard work over the years. He told her what a good job she had done and what a good mate she had been.

However, the Holy Spirit gave me insight and totally changed my thinking. This scripture does not say anything about the virtuous woman dying. It simply says her children, as they were rising up, or as the Strong's Exhaustive Concordance of the Bible states it, "becoming powerful or coming on the scene" began to call her blessed[1]. Her children knew she was empowered by God, and they recognized the power that resonated from her life. Her husband had long praised her sitting in the gates, or in other words, he bragged about her all over town. The virtuous woman was loved and praised by her family because she was the same powerful woman at home that she was in the community. If your children are calling you blessed and your husband is praising you, you have accomplished more than one could ever know.

This woman did not put on a holy act at church and act like the devil at home. I have often taught, "You are who you are at home, not at church. Your true nature is that which you display in your home." This woman of Proverbs 31 met the standard and surpassed it.

If we are enthusiastic about life and we live purposefully and intentionally, others are able to capture our vitality and energy and reflect happiness. When we are sad and depressed, our children mirror that as well. As a counselor I advise parents that if they think their children need counseling, to first seek counseling for themselves and then seek counseling with their children.

At times children reflect parental weaknesses. If the parents seek help and get on a healthy path emotionally and mentally, the children will soon follow. Just as an airline flight attendant ask parents to put the oxygen mask on themselves first and then on their child. First, get the help you need, then you are much more likely to be able to help your children.

The Proverbs 31 woman not only impressed her home, but also her community. She greatly impacted her community, and they also admired her. The community did not see a fake woman, but a woman who was consistent, genuine, loving, and powerful. She was the same everywhere she went with everyone she met—a woman of virtue.

Give her of the fruit of her hands; and let her own works praise her in the gates. Proverbs 31:31

An important principle found in this last verse of Proverbs 31 is that of appreciation and recognition. As we see the accomplishments of women, instead of down playing their successes or becoming jealous and envious of them, the Bible teaches to give these women the praise they so gallantly deserve. Through recognizing and praising the accomplishments of others, we show honor. We become inspired to be more diligent in our endeavors and all women are encouraged to work harder toward accomplishing goals.

Recently, I applied for graduate school at Florida State University. After three years I finished all the credit hours and internships to receive my master's degree. One of my professors asked me if I was going to go through the formal graduation ceremony and "walk the stage." I told him I really felt too old to "walk" with all the younger college-aged students, but he encouraged me to participate in the formal service. He said that it is important to take time and celebrate the achievements in our lives.

I took his advice and bought my cap and gown. I'm glad I did. At the commencement, several older women in the community expressed to me their admiration of my achievement and explained that they were inspired to return to school and finish their degrees. I am so glad that I was not only able to commemorate what I had worked so hard for, but also I was able to influence others.

God believes in rewards. The Bible says He rewards those who remain faithful and those who overcome, and He will give them white raiment and make them to sit with Him on His throne. Matthew 16:27 says God shall reward everyman according to his works.

We can expect rewards from God because Hebrews 11:6 tells us that God is a rewarder of those who diligently seek Him. It's His delight to reward your life. Hopefully, we can draw off His character and be delighted when we see others praised for their efforts and accomplishments. In the "old days" we were taught to congratulate those who won awards, even if we were competing with them because it was a matter of honor.

Jesus mentioned that things done in secret would be rewarded openly. We need not wonder why some people are rewarded so fantastically. Evidently in their private lives, they are obeying God. For example, the Bible says when we pray secretly, God will reward us openly. As we give alms secretly, God rewards us openly. Let us not be envious of those who reap rewards from God, but let their examples provoke us to good works. Give them the praise that they rightly deserve and applaud their works. It does us good to rejoice with those who are rejoicing.

The virtuous woman deserves what her determination and discipline obtained for her. The Lord exhorts us to give her of the fruit of her hands and let her own works praise her. Of course He does not want us lifted up in pride, but He does desire that we be recognized for our efforts and properly rewarded.

God is a good God—and *God loves women!*

References

[1] Strong's Exhaustive Concordance of the Bible, James Strong, Abingden Press, 1890.

[2] Source Obained from the Internet: (International Gemstone Association, Online).

[4]The Gatekeepers, Nathanel Wolf, Rhema Bible Church, 2005.

[3]A.C. Nielsen, 1998.

[5] Who Said Women Can't Teach?, Charles Trombley, Bridge Publishing, Inc., 1985.

[6] Source Obtained from the Internet: www.brainyquote.com/ quotes/authors/m/mary_day_ash.html.

[7]Marriage and Families, 5th Edition, Nijole Benokraitis, Pearson Prentice Hall, 2005, p. 274.

[8]Total Fitness and Wellness, Scott K. Powers, Stephen L. Dodd, Virtinia J. Noland, Pearson   Benjamin Cummings, California, 2006.

[9]Source Obtained from the Internet: (Centers for Disease Control and Prevention)

[10]Daughter of Destiny, Jamie Buckingham, Logos, International, 1976.

Salvation Prayer

If you want to accept Jesus as your Lord and Savior please pray this: *God, I come to you and ask you to forgive me of sin. I give my life to you. According to Romans 10:9 and 10, I believe you raised Jesus from the dead and I confess Jesus is my Lord. I am now a new creature in Christ Jesus. Thank you Father for making me born again. In Jesus Name I pray, Amen.*

Contact Us

For more information or for a list of other materials available by Scarlett Harrington, please write:

Goodness of God Church

P.O. Box 19495

Panama City Beach, Florida 32417

Or visit **www.goodnessofgodchurch.com**